Gender and Governance

THE GENDER LENS SERIES

Series Editors

Judith A. Howard
University of Washington

Barbara Risman
North Carolina State University

Joey Sprague
University of Kansas

The Gender Lens series has been conceptualized as a way of encouraging the development of a sociological understanding of gender. A "gender lens" means working to make gender visible in social phenomena; asking if, how, and why social processes, standards, and opportunities differ systematically for women and men. It also means recognizing that gender inequality is inextricably braided with other systems of inequality. The Gender Lens series is committed to social change directed toward eradicating these inequalities. Originally published by Sage Publications and Pine Forge Press, all Gender Lens books are now available from AltaMira Press.

BOOKS IN THE SERIES

Yen Le Espiritu, *Asian American Women and Men: Labor, Laws, and Love*

Judith A. Howard and Jocelyn A. Hollander, *Gendered Situations, Gendered Selves: A Gender Lens on Social Psychology*

Michael A. Messner, *Politics of Masculinities: Men in Movements*

Judith Lorber and Lisa Jean Moore, *Gender and the Social Construction of Illness*, Second Edition

Scott Coltrane, *Gender and Families*

Myra Marx Ferree, Judith Lorber, and Beth B. Hess, editors, *Revisioning Gender*

Pepper Schwartz and Virginia Rutter, *The Gender of Sexuality: Exploring Sexual Possibilities*

Francesca M. Cancian and Stacey J. Oliker, *Caring and Gender*

M. Bahati Kuumba, *Gender and Social Movements*

Toni M. Calasanti and Kathleen F. Slevin, *Gender, Social Inequalities, and Aging*

Gender and Governance

Lisa D. Brush

ALTAMIRA
PRESS
A Division of
ROWMAN & LITTLEFIELD PUBLISHERS, INC.
Walnut Creek • Lanham • New York • Toronto • Oxford

ALTAMIRA PRESS
A Division of Rowman & Littlefield Publishers, Inc.
1630 North Main Street, #367
Walnut Creek, CA 94596
www.altamirapress.com

Rowman & Littlefield Publishers, Inc.
A wholly owned subsidiary of the Rowman & Littlefield Publishing Group, Inc.
4501 Forbes Boulevard, Suite 200
Lanham, MD 20706

PO Box 317
Oxford
OX2 9RU, UK

British Library Cataloguing in Publication Information Available

Library of Congress Cataloging-in-Publication Data

Brush, Lisa Diane.
  Gender and governance / Lisa D. Brush.
      p.   cm.—(The gender lens series)
  Includes bibliographical references and index.
  ISBN 0-7591-0141-8 (cloth : alk. paper)—ISBN 0-7591-0142-6 (pbk. : alk. paper)
      1. Power (Social sciences).   2. State, The.   3. Feminism.   4. Civil society—United States.   5. Civil society—Europe, Western.   6. United States—Social policy.   7. Europe, Western—Social policy.   I. Title.   II. Series.

  JC330.B75   2003
  303.3—dc21   2003008501

Printed in the United States of America

⊗ ™ The paper used in this publication meets the minimum requirements of American National Standard for Information Sciences—Permanence of Paper for Printed Library Materials, ANSI/NISO Z39.48-1992.

CONTENTS

It is now more than twenty years since feminist sociologists identified gender as an important analytic dimension in sociology. In the intervening decades, theory and research on gender have grown exponentially. With this series, we intend to further this scholarship, as well as ensure that theory and research on gender become fully integrated into the discipline as a whole.

In a classic edited collection, Beth Hess and Myra Marx Ferree (1987) identify three stages in the study of women and men since 1970. Initially, the emphasis was on sex differences and the extent to which such differences might be based in biological properties of individuals. In the second stage, the focus shifted to the individual sex roles and socialization, exposing gender as the product of specific social arrangements, although still conceptualizing it as an individual trait. The hallmark of the third stage is the recognition of the centrality of gender as an organizing principle in all social systems, including work, politics, everyday interaction, families, economic development, law, education, and a host of other social domains. As our understanding of gender has become more social, so has our awareness that gender is experienced and organized in race- and class-specific ways.

In the summer of 1992, the American Sociological Association (ASA) funded a small conference, organized by Barbara Risman and Joey Sprague, to discuss the evolution of gender in these distinctly sociological frameworks. The conference brought together a sampling of gender scholars working in a wide range of substantive areas with a diversity of methods to focus on gender as a principle of social organization. The discussions of the state of feminist scholarship made it clear that gender is pervasive in society and operates at multiple levels. Gender shapes identities and perception, interactional practices, and the very forms of social institutions, and it does so in race- and class-specific ways. If we did not see gender in social phenomena, we were not seeing them clearly.

The participants in the ASA-sponsored seminar recognized that although these developing ideas about gender were widely accepted by feminist sociologists and many others who study social inequalities, they were relatively unfamiliar to many who work within other sociological paradigms. This book series was conceived at that conference as a means of introducing these ideas to sociological colleagues and students, and of helping to develop gender scholarship further.

As series editors, we feel it is time for gender scholars to speak to our colleagues and to the general education of students. There are many sociologists and scholars in other social sciences who want to incorporate scholarship on gender and its intersections with race, class, and sexuality in their teaching and research, but lack the tools to do so. For those who have not worked in this area, the prospect of the bibliographic research necessary to develop supplementary units, or to transform their own teaching and scholarship, is daunting. Moreover, the publications necessary to penetrate a curriculum resistant to change and encumbered by inertia have simply not been available. We conceptualize this book series as a way of meeting the needs of these scholars, and thereby also encouraging the development of the sociological understanding of gender by offering a "gender lens."

What do we mean by a *gender lens*? We mean working to make gender visible in social phenomena, asking if, how, and why social processes, standards, and opportunities differ systematically in women and men. We also mean recognizing that gender inequality is inextricably intertwined with other systems of inequity. Looking at the world through a gendered lens thus implies two seemingly contradictory tasks. First, it means unpacking the assumptions about gender that pervade sociological research and social life more generally. At the same time, looking through a gender lens means showing just how central assumptions about gender continue to be to the organization of the social world, regardless of their empirical reality. We show how our often unquestioned ideas about gender affect the worlds we see, the questions we ask, the answers we envision. The Gender Lens series is committed to social change directed toward eradicating these inequalities. Our goals are consistent with initiatives at colleges and universities across the United States that are encouraging the development of more diverse scholarship and teaching.

The books in the Gender Lens series are aimed at different audiences and have been written for a variety of uses, from assigned readings in introductory undergraduate courses to graduate seminars, and as professional resources for our colleagues. The series includes several different styles of books that address these goals in distinct ways. We are excited about the series and anticipate that it will have an enduring impact on the direction of both pedagogy and scholarship in sociology and other related social sciences. We invite you, the reader, to join us in thinking through these difficult but exciting issues by offering feedback or developing your own project and proposing it to us for the series.

About This Volume

In writing the current volume, Lisa Brush took seriously our brief to imagine what political sociology, state theory, and welfare state studies would look like if they fully integrated insights from feminist scholarship. Her central innovation is powerful in its simplicity. She urges readers to understand feminist political sociology and state theory by viewing states and social policies through two facets of a gender lens. She inspects what she calls the *governance of gender,* that is, how states and social policies produce and police the boundaries between masculinity and femininity and thus enforce or undermine male privilege in everyday life. She also investigates what she calls the *gender of governance,* that is, the ways assumptions and practices of gender difference and dominance organize the institutions, capacities, and ideologies of governance.

Brush's synthesis of the complex literatures on gender, states, and social policies makes sophisticated research and theory accessible to nonspecialists. Her argument also advances debates among feminist scholars on several frontiers. In particular, Brush weaves through the book an important argument about including violence against women among the notions of "gender" and "welfare" that are the conceptual bedrock of feminist welfare-state studies.

The book starts off with an introductory section that provides the conceptual foundation for looking at gender, states, and social policies through a gender lens. Brush then guides readers through a review of empirical evidence (focused primarily on the welfare states of the North Atlantic capitalist democracies, especially the United States) of how states govern gender and how gender organizes governance. In the final section, Brush examines the implications of her approach for feminist theory and politics, and builds on the conceptual and empirical foundations of the book to argue for further feminist innovations in welfare state studies and state theory. Throughout, Brush presents a strong—and readable—case for why students, scholars, and other readers should share her passion for feminist political sociology.

Judith A. Howard
Barbara Risman
Joey Sprague

A C K N O W L E D G M E N T S

As with any book close to two decades in the making, the roots of this work are deep and tangled. So are my debts. Phil Brenner, intrepid leader of the American University Foreign Policy Semester and Semester in London programs that I attended as a sophomore and junior in college, introduced me to the joys of historical materialism. He and Rich Hiskes, chair of the senior thesis I completed as University Scholar at the University of Connecticut, encouraged my earliest forays into marxist and feminist theories of politics and the state. For more years than either of us care to admit, Myra Marx Ferree (who followed me from the University of Connecticut to the University of Wisconsin, Madison) has provided mentoring that has been a model of feminist scholarly capacity building. Myra, Rich, and Phil encouraged me to study class analysis and historical change with Erik Olin Wright, who relished reinforcing my worst structuralist tendencies. Erik, Pam Oliver, Chas Camic, Ann Shola Orloff, and Linda Gordon (all then at Madison) oversaw my protracted research apprenticeship and nurtured the kernel of what became this book. My brief postdoctoral stint as a policy wonk at the Rockefeller Foundation helped me define feminist policy critique, and Peter Goldmark and Julia Lopez inspired me to lead, follow, or get out of the way. Katherine Holmsen has known how to comfort and challenge me across time, distance, and discipline. Rebekah Michaels first put into my head the notion that I might write a book someday. Jane Larson encouraged me to cultivate old-fashioned virtues and to value grace. Jane's pride and pleasure in my accomplishments sustained me. It is to the high standards to which they all have held me over many years that I happily attribute the intellectual contribution I seek to make in this book.

Most recently, I owe thanks for help and inspiration to Julia Adams, Delia Aguilar, Kathy Blee, Karen Christopher, Myra Marx Ferree, Val Jenness, Leslie McCall, Martha McCluskey and Carl Nightengale, Wendy Mink, Ted Muller, Karín Aguilar San Juan and Tracy Ore, Mimi Schippers (may we enjoy many more years as babes behaving badly!), and Laurel Weldon and Aaron Hoffman.

I am incredibly fortunate to be a social scientist in a writing group with three English Ph.D.s. Thanks to Carol Stabile, Carol Mason, and Nancy Glazener for sharing the rewards of hard work, mutual respect, and strong norms of reciprocity.

Two anonymous reviewers for the Gender Lens series provided detailed comments that pushed me to strengthen my argument. Many thanks to the Gender Lens series editors, and to publisher Mitch Allen, who taught me under duress that a book manuscript doesn't have to be perfect, it just has to be finished. Judy Howard commented on material that became the last two chapters at the ASA meetings in 2001 and on the first complete version as "second editor," prompting many revisions. Barbara Risman gave me a push by announcing my work in progress at the 2002 Winter Meetings of Sociologists for Women in Society in New Orleans. Words fail to acknowledge the contribution of my Gender Lens "manuscript midwife," Joey Sprague. Revisioning feminist scholarship while reconstructing the basic areas of sociological inquiry is a tall order. I am delighted to be able to contribute to the editors' lofty goals.

Special appreciation to Amy Elman, dear feminist friend and critic. Amy commented on uncountable versions with her characteristic patience, humor, integrity, generosity, and graciousness.

Caroline Cunningham, Carolyn Gatty, Amelia Haviland, Ellen K. Scott, Yael Seligman, Suzanna Danuta Walters, and Morgan Wolf encouraged me to pick myself up, dust myself off, and start all over again— sometimes quite literally. Elizabeth French has patiently listened to my ideas for two decades. Judy Klempner has been a true friend since I was most broken. Jon and Carrie helped me rediscover my great capacity for silliness. Kathryn Collins and Connie Oxford were foremost among the many people who cared for me when head injuries and painkillers disrupted everything. Pat Bartone and Robin Barack accompanied me through the uncharted territory of trauma and recovery, and Kelly Happe, Jamie Phillips, and Tom Rens rode through it with me. Alison Krauss, Carrie Newcomer, and the singularly amazing Erika Luckett—who has a song not just in her heart but in every fiber of her being—provided the soundtrack.

The Faculty of Arts and Sciences at the University of Pittsburgh supported a semester of medical leave and a research sabbatical, and provided me with the means of intellectual production. Patrick Doreian, my department chair during the years this manuscript was under contract, commented on early versions of several chapters and arranged my medical leave and sabbatical.

My faithful "interested nonspecialist" readers/listeners include Alan H. Brush, Karen Drescher Flora (who edited the entire manuscript on an extremely tight schedule), Amelia Haviland, and Rickie Solinger. You laugh at my jokes and remind me why I love what I do—what author could ask for anything more?

The Rube Goldberg machine illustrated in chapter 1 is reproduced with permission of Rube Goldberg, Inc.

Versions of arguments I make here and some of the evidence I discuss appeared in several other publications, including:

"The curious courtship of feminist jurisprudence and feminist state theory: Smart on the power of law." *Law & Social Inquiry* 19 (1994): 1059–1077. Parts of this essay appear in chapter 6. Reprinted with permission from the University of Chicago Press.

"Harm, moralism, and the struggle for the soul of feminism." *Violence Against Women* 3 (1997): 237–256. Parts of this essay appear in chapter 6. Reprinted with permission of Sage Publications.

"Changing the subject: Gender and welfare regimes." *Social Politics* 9 (2002): 161–186. Revised parts of this essay appear in chapter 5. Reprinted with permission of Oxford University Press.

"Gender and the uses of history." *Journal of Urban History* 29 (2003): 216–225. Revised parts of this essay appear in chapters 3 and 4. Reprinted with permission of Sage Publications.

A note on style: Double quotation marks (". . .") denote the enclosed text as a direct quotation from another text or speaker. Single quotation marks ('. . .') distinguish the enclosed text as everyday or expert speech. Text in *italics* signals emphasis, indicates words in a language other than English (as in *liberté*), or marks the title of a book (Hobbes's *Leviathan*) or text in the public domain (bumper stickers, for example).

February 2003/Adar I 5763
Pittsburgh, Pennsylvania

 וטהר לבנו לעבדך באמת

Strengthen our hearts that we may serve in truth.

PART 1

Gender, States, and Social Policies

CHAPTER 1

Where the Power Is

There is an old joke about Willie Sutton, a wise guy who, when asked why he robbed banks, answered, "That's where the money is." The punch line motivates my writing a book viewing states and social policies through a gender lens: *States are where the power is.*

Willie Sutton's observation about the concentration of cash in banks is common sense. It is likewise common sense for social scientists, lawyers, pundits, voters, reformers, and revolutionaries to assume that power is concentrated in states. Of course, power, like money, is everywhere. Willie Sutton could have picked pockets, snatched purses, or fished for stray coins through a sewer grate with a wad of chewing gum on the end of a string. But in a bank heist, the potential cash rewards are much greater than pocket change. The concentration of money in banks made them worthy of Willie Sutton's larcenous ambitions even though security measures are more daunting for burglars at the local savings and loan than for muggers in a back alley.

I refer to something similar when I assert that *States are where the power is.* People are acting powerfully when they make meaning, mobilize for collective or individual action, persuade or coerce, constrain or enable, move others to hope or pity, make and accept or reject claims on resources, establish or contest order, enforce sanctions to reward or punish. These are ubiquitous human activities. At the level of small change, people do them everywhere, all the time. But like banks with cash, states are privileged sites for power.

For example, states and social policies shape how people think and act. The decisions and actions of bureaucrats, civil servants, legislators, social workers, judges, teachers, police officers, and military generals influence people's life chances. The relations of rule set people's capacities to rebel and create the possibilities for social change. In theory, democratic states are one of the ways "we the people" govern ourselves. Governing is an important life activity, an endless source of worthwhile tasks and challenges to human intelligence and creativity, and a potential avenue to justice. States are us, not in some mystical sense but because states and social policies are historical, social, human institutions.

Even in societies ideologically committed to laissez-faire—the notion that the state that governs best, governs least—state powers enforce and delimit the economic and interpersonal opportunities we may exploit and the risks we must run. States provide the preconditions (property, contract, copyright, legal tender) for establishing 'free' markets in land, labor, information, and capital. State power, often through law, sets and maintains the conditions of exchanges and alliances, be they financial, cultural, sexual, or familial. States and social policies mobilize, recognize, and rebuff citizens and their claims. State institutions and capacities both constitute and distribute resources for popular and elite struggles. By studying patterns of politics and state institution building, observers can answer crucial questions about the organization and dynamics of societies and about the lives of those included and excluded as citizens.

States and social policies influence everyday life. They establish tax rates and exemptions, and determine whether tax revenues pay for bombers or elementary schools, health care or interest on the national debt. It matters whether local rulers are beholden to local residents, local or distant corporations, or imperial conquerors. Payroll deductions may insure income security for the unemployed or for corporate investors. Welfare policy may establish a safety net for single mothers or for financial speculators, for people who are old or infirm or for hedge fund operators. States and social policies help determine whether or not you have redress against workplace grievances. States can send you, your siblings, or your children to war. People can turn to states when they are sick, hungry, abused, homeless, or out of work. Social policies can guarantee or deny people access to potable water, affordable child care, and abortion services. States determine who can marry, and whether marriage is necessary in order to legitimate your relationship, your child custody claim, your sexual activity, your child's birthright, and your access to work permits, housing, credit, and health care.

States and social policies also determine the limits and possibilities of collective struggle. States establish the degree of 'say' vulnerable members of the population have in decisions that affect the physical safety, environmental sustainability, economic viability, degree of inequality, and civil quality of life where they reside and work. States can direct the money people try to save for their retirement or for their children's education to finance speculation, or to capitalize local employment and infrastructure. States may draw civilian and military leaders, jurists, legislators, and bureaucrats from a broad spectrum of society or from a narrow elite. Social policies constitute or challenge business as usual. Law and social policy can recognize and redress harms to people's well-being, or support profit, property, expertise, masculinity, and racial-ethnic privilege. Must the buyer beware? Can you—and people who vehemently disagree with you—meaningfully criticize business as usual without fear of arrest or torture? Do the police protect persons or property? These are central empirical questions of how states shape the common life.

State guarantees of privacy can foster diverse, flourishing communities and protect the integrity of individual decisions about worship, education, sexuality, relationships, pregnancy, and child rearing. On the other hand, a veil of privacy may protect union-busting employers, bigots, wife beaters, child abusers, pornographers, and pimps. The division of public and private that counters totalitarianism can render invisible the work that some people do. Separating the personal from the political hides the harms of violence, sexual exploitation, and women's subordination. Issues of privacy such as these are especially contradictory, potentially contentious, and therefore useful when discussing states and social policy in the liberal democracies of the North Atlantic that are the primary focus of this book.

The notion that *states are where the power is* rests on the distinction between a private zone of individuality and freedom and a public realm of collectivity and subordination. In this model, commonly called *liberalism*, the realm of individuality and freedom—that is, *civil society*—has its own 'natural laws' of supply and demand, diminishing returns, group formation, honor and duty, and survival of the fittest. The realm of collective deliberation and submission—that is, the state—institutes the rule of law, bureaucratic procedure, administrative capacity, and political reason. Ironically for neoclassical liberalism, it is state enforcement of constraints (such as contract) that makes 'free' (in the sense of unfettered) trade and labor possible. Liberal reasoning is utterly taken for granted in the countries I focus on in this book, most especially in the United States.

In liberal countries, states are where the power is because power inheres in the public (as opposed to private) and the political (as opposed to the 'state of nature'). I discuss the division between public and private as a feature of liberal states and social policies in chapter 4.

In this book, I discuss the extent to which liberal states contribute to or merely reflect civil society. I am particularly interested in states and social policies as 'where the power is,' and in strategies for feminist political rebels. In chapters 3 and 4, I analyze the ways states and social policies construct gendered notions of citizenship and worthiness, discipline women and men into conformity, and provoke and channel resistance. In chapter 5 and especially chapter 6, I conclude by grappling directly with the strategic problem of whether feminists ought to abandon states and social policies as terrains of struggle that are irredeemably hostile to efforts to promote democracy, social justice, and women's emancipation.

States and social policies do not have to be the *only* site of power in order to be analyzed as one important place where at least *some* power—some capacity to make meaning, establish and enforce rules of conduct and commerce—is. Therefore, it is worthwhile for feminists to struggle over politics, states, and social policies, just as it made sense for Willie Sutton to rob banks.

What Are States and Social Policies?

When I refer to *states*, I refer to what French political theorist Louis Althusser (1971) called an *apparatus of rule* associated with a national territory. The apparatus of rule is made up of institutions, capacities, and ideologies. The apparatus of rule includes a set of *institutions*, such as legislatures, courts, civil and welfare service bureaucracies, prisons, schools, armies, navies, and police forces. The apparatus of rule also encompasses juridical, military and paramilitary, administrative, and therapeutic *capacities* (Fraser 1989). That is, the state can authoritatively impose specific ways of making and enforcing the law and legal decisions. States control crime and punishment, including the death penalty. States monopolize making war, protecting—and taxing—property, and keeping whatever passes for peace. Strong states effectively implement policy, whether that means they make the trains run on time or maintain racial segregation, provide for the poor or harass the indigent, foster cooperation or defend local and expand global interests in territory and commerce. States define and protect public health and rehabilitation. State officials determine who is sick or crazy, and states license the experts empowered to diagnose, treat, and quarantine. In addition, each national apparatus of rule entails a characteristic cluster of *ideologies*. That is, the realities of political institutions and capacities generate concomitant sets of ideas and ways of talking about how politics and power operate, such as the rule of law, manifest destiny, universal manhood suffrage, and family values.

A specific apparatus of rule looks more like a Rube Goldberg machine than a finely tuned instrument of social control. Mismatched parts and spandrels with obsolete or unknown purposes appear cobbled together or overly complicated

Moreover, unlike a lathe or an internal combustion engine, not all of what I mean by the state or the national apparatus of rule is tangible. For example, *war machine* is shorthand for one part of the apparatus of rule. The war machine is the "military-industrial complex" to which U.S. president Eisenhower (1960) referred, and more. The war machine combines military and civilian personnel, institutions (in the United States, from West Point to the Pentagon to the National Security Council), and hardware (guns, tanks, and aircraft carriers) and software (such as the Internet, which was developed with funding from the U.S. Department of Defense). The war machine consists of assembly lines and shipyards, profits and paperwork, as well as rhetoric about justice and honor, injury and righteousness. Leaders in politics, commerce, and 'research and development' invoke the war machine to mobilize literal and figurative support for conquest and killing. The war machine marshals the resources for making war, in part, as feminist political scientist Cynthia Enloe (2000) shows, by militarizing everyday life (see also Goldstein 2001). Beyond capitol rotunda and ballot boxes, tanks and traffic cops, states are about ideas. Ideas can be almost as devastating and as difficult to dodge as bullets, if somewhat less predictable in their trajectories and effects.

'The state' is an apparatus of rule; it is an organization, not an agent. People can build state institutions, use state capacities, and produce and take advantage of political ideologies. But 'the state' cannot act. It is easy to point to the *effects* of the state—highways and potholes, public schools and low test scores, or subsidized medical care and high prices for prescription drugs. It is simple to point to the *symbols* of the state—flags, constitutions, or presidential motorcades. But it can be hard to pin down 'the state' as something bounded and concrete. Nevertheless, this "supreme public power within a sovereign political entity" (the definition of

Pencil Sharpener

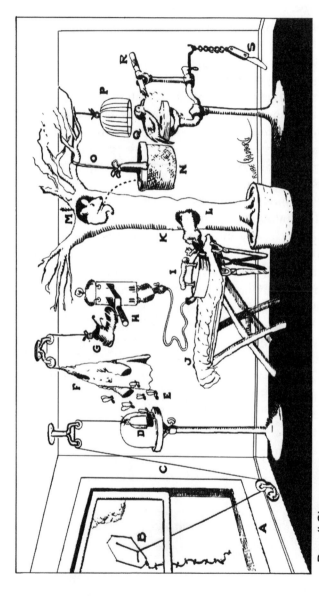

The Professor gets his think-tank working and evolves the simplified pencil sharpener.

Open window (A) and fly kite (B). String (C) lifts small door (D), allowing moths (E) to escape and eat red flannel shirt (F). As weight of shirt becomes less, shoe (G) steps on switch (H) which heats electric iron (I) and burns hole in pants (J).

Smoke (K) enters hole in tree (L), smoking out opossum (M) which jumps into basket (N), pulling rope (O) and lifting cage (P), allowing woodpecker (Q) to chew wood from pencil (R), exposing lead. Emergency knife (S) is always handy in case opossum or the woodpecker gets sick and can't work.

state in my *American Heritage Dictionary*) is sufficiently real in its consequences, and in the minds of those people who give it a moment's
thought, to be the object of social scientific and feminist inquiry.

Moreover, 'the state' may be meaningfully modified to specify historical combinations of institutions, capacities, and ideologies. The apparatus
of rule might be contingent, temporary, and highly unstable. But it makes
sense to distinguish a hereditary absolutist monarchy from a fascist dictatorship—each is a very different apparatus of rule. It also makes sense to
use modifiers to locate 'the state' in a particular set of power relations in
civil society. For example, there are discernible, meaningful differences
among a capitalist parliamentary state, a colonial mercantilist state, and
a revolutionary populist state. Different institutions, capacities, and ideologies—and experiences of politics and everyday life—are involved in rule
by a military junta, by a clerical assembly, or by a workers' council.

In this book, I am primarily concerned with the apparatus of rule in
Western capitalist democracies in the twentieth century: the welfare state.
The institutions, capacities, and ideologies characteristic of welfare states
are consonant with modest political interventions to remedy the inequalities and hazards of capitalism (and more rarely, sexism and racism). Welfare states provide cash and in-kind benefits, subsidies, and services.
They regulate wages and labor standards, air and water quality, land use
and media broadcasting. Politicians and administrators generally build
and support welfare states in the wake of crises in employment and
profitability, in response to calls for a 'safety net' for the poor, out of fear
of massive social unrest or revolution, and in response to international
threats to domestic security. The extent and generosity of welfare benefits
vary over time and across countries because they depend at least as much
on politics and demands from social movements as they depend on economics and the level of resources available to "provide for the common
welfare."

The institutions, capacities, and ideologies of welfare states vary considerably across the countries of western Europe and North America. The
United States has a comparatively laggard, underdeveloped welfare state.
The United States is exceptional even among the 'liberal' welfare states
(such as Canada, the United Kingdom, and Australia; see O'Connor, Orloff, and Shaver 1999) where state institutions, capacities, and ideologies
supporting egalitarian intervention are puny compared to those in 'social
democratic' welfare states (such as Denmark, Finland, and Sweden; for

the classic comparison of these and other European welfare states, see Esping-Andersen 1990; 1999).

Although they are my main concern here, welfare states are not the only type of state that thrived in western Europe in the twentieth century. Fascist states, characterized by totalitarian institutions, capacities, and ideologies of extreme militarized authoritarianism, paternalism, and racism, were the apparatus of rule in Spain under the dictatorship of Franco, in France under Pétain, in Italy under Mussolini, and in Germany's Third Reich. Moreover, beyond the boundaries of western Europe and North America, state socialism, colonial states, and other constellations of institutions, capacities, and ideologies abounded during the twentieth century. (I refer readers interested in this much wider variation in the apparatus of rule around the world to the excellent and growing comparative and global literature on states. See the suggested readings for this and other chapters at the end of the book.)

When I refer to *social policies*, I mean the set of enacted (if not explicit) guidelines for decisions and actions by state actors. Social policies may be coherent across domains and consistent within them—or not. For instance, policies on zoning may augment or diminish policies on environmental protection. Policies on trade, taxation, and social provision may reinforce or undermine policies regulating business, labor, and economic development. Policies on marriage and family may contradict or complement policies on immigration and civil rights. Policies on abortion may be at odds or consistent with policies on maternal and child welfare, equality, and medical services. Policies on 'vice' may encourage, prohibit, or merely regulate sexual exploitation, protection rackets, gambling, civilian access to firearms, and drug traffic.

In any particular case, the coherence of social policies within and between substantive areas, while unlikely, is an empirical question. Nevertheless, the apparent overall 'fit' between state institutions, capacities, and ideologies (on the one hand) and the content of social policies (on the other) is a convenient indicator for classifying and assessing political power. It is a different experience to live in a police state, a warfare state, a welfare state, or a workfare state. It is fairly easy to trace at least some of those experiential differences in terms of social policies.

Gender, States, and Social Policies

Like states and social policies, gender is about power. Through gender relations, people continually recreate and reinforce the distinction between masculinity and femininity. Through gender relations, people police variations within masculinity and femininity. That is, gender is about drawing a clear, bright line between men and women. Gender is also about punishing and rewarding individuals according to the degree to which they stay within the boundaries of 'acting like a lady' or 'taking it like a man' that are deemed appropriate for someone of their race, class, and nationality. Collective and individual actions bolster or undermine male dominance and female subordination. People, institutions, and practices privilege masculinity as universal and thereby render femininity deviant and feminism ideological. In other words, through gender, people make meanings, collectively organize, establish subject locations, persuade and coerce, make and accept or reject claims on resources, and establish social order. Gender is an exercise of power, which privileges (some) men and (many varieties of) masculinity at the expense of women and femininity, some individuals and forms more than others. Gender is a system of power relations, and a way of signaling or signifying power.

Gender organizes power at the level of individuals. Consider what it signals to say someone has been 'emasculated' in an interpersonal interaction. Note the difference between the grudging respect we might accord a powerful man ('bastard' though we might call him) and the vengeful disdain often reserved for an equally powerful woman (labeled a 'bitch'). Contemplate the fate of an intersex infant (one born with ambiguous genitalia) and the 'heroic' efforts of surgery and socialization that parents, doctors, and state officials will undertake in order to contain the wide array of human bodies into just two opposite, internally homogeneous categories. Gender power organizes seemingly 'natural' bodies, born with seemingly obvious sexual dimorphism, into the exaggerated masculinity of Arnold Schwarzenegger and femininity of Dolly Parton. At the individual level, gender is more than just pink and blue in the bassinet. The distinctions associated with gender result from two forms of hard work. The first is what French sociologist Pierre Bourdieu called the "long collective labor of socialization" (2001, p. 3): all the assumptions and training that go into differentiating masculine from feminine. The second, as Bourdieu pointed out, is the work of erasing the traces of all the social labor required to make gender look natural (and therefore compulsory, universal, and unchanging) as individuals live it out in their bodies, beliefs, and interactions.

Gender also organizes power at the level of complex institutions. Think of the gendered division of labor in corporations, with masculine boardrooms and feminine clerical support. Take, for example, the gendered distinctions between doctors and nurses, judges and paralegals, construction workers and waitresses, war correspondents and gossip columnists. Gender saturates the different spaces, skills, and authority associated with these occupations and with institutions such as law, health care, and the media. In terms of the apparatus of rule and state institutions, capacities, and ideologies (the focus of this book), consider the gendered definition, in the Defense of Marriage Act signed by President Clinton, of marriage as the union of one man and one woman. Consider the stakes in the question of allowing women in the armed forces, or of allowing female soldiers, sailors, or pilots to participate in combat—a prerequisite for reaching the heights of military command. Note as well the gendered characteristics of 'statesmanship' or 'brinkmanship,' and the power of worry over the 'wimp' factor in presidential politics.

Power in general and state power in particular is never neutral or neuter. *The principal argument of this book is that states and social policies are gendered.* That is, states and social policies reproduce, and are inflected with, masculinity and femininity as different and unequal markers of power. Sociologists Ann Oakley and Alan Rigby note that "neither the welfare state, nor welfare services, nor the informal provision of welfare within the family and community can be understood in terms of an ungendered scenario" (1998, p. 103). As comparative political sociologists Julia O'Connor, Ann Orloff, and Sheila Shaver put it: "Gender relations cannot be understood apart from the state, politics and policy; states influence gender relations, and are in turn influenced by gender relations" (1999, p. 10).

The mutual influences of states and gender relations are generally underanalyzed. Political scientists Georgia Duerst-Lahti and Rita Mae Kelly note that analysts "become distracted by sex differences, or more accurately, how women are different from the norm men set" (1995, p. 265). As a consequence, social scientists frequently end up trying to explain away marginal sex differences in, say, voting patterns (known as the 'gender gap' but really just a way of talking about how women differ from the masculine norm), rather than analyzing the double standard of leadership that requires women to "overcompensate to demonstrate that they are assimilated to compulsory masculinity" (p. 266). The universalist pretenses of masculinism can make it hard to see gender and the power relations it constitutes.

Feminism—specifically, using a gender lens—is all about perceiving and working to change gendered power relations. Using a gender lens, in the words of the Gender Lens series editors, "means working to make gender visible in social phenomena, asking if, how, and why social processes, standards, and opportunities differ systematically for women and men" (1998, p. x). The advantages of the gender lens metaphor for feminist investigations are many. It is a reminder of the social character of gender difference and male dominance. After all, a lens is the product of human design and action. A lens is manufactured in the context of social relations of production.

Anyone who wears glasses knows a lens provides a powerful corrective, and can completely change the way you view things. In the context of a history of social science that has consistently silenced and excluded women and feminist critiques of power, such a corrective is a vital tool. Moreover, lenses change perception, even if they are not corrective. Think of the expression 'looking at the world through rose-colored glasses', which evokes an overly optimistic way of seeing. Or recall the pattern of dark patches on a car windshield made of polarized glass—only visible if you, too, are wearing polarized sunglasses. The optical properties that a person wearing polarized sunglasses perceives in the car windshield are there whether she looks or not, whether her glasses are polarized or not. Similarly, gender and its structural effects are there whether we use a gender lens to look at states and social policies or not. The lens just makes the perception possible—and much more likely.

Finally, the gender lens metaphor helps present intuitively the critical notion that *experiences, point of view,* and *interests* (acknowledged or unconscious) shape perceptions. Choices of question, method, sources, analytic strategy, and style of presentation are colored by social location and power, including gender. You can look *at* a lens, and describe its properties and effects, instead of only looking *through* it without noticing the particular vision of the world it makes possible. This alienable quality of a lens—the ability to take glasses off and look them over—makes it a particularly good metaphor for a set of historically specific, socially constructed ways of seeing and being such as gender.

The lens metaphor also has some drawbacks for feminist purposes. It might imply that there is some unmediated way of looking at the world, that there is a naturalistic, value-free way to understand states and social policies without the 'bias' of critical approaches. In the case of gender, having to use a corrective lens implies that universalism and neutrality are possible, desirable, and not at odds with 'normal.' Many people consider some aspects of gender—specifically male dominance—to be normal, neutral, and universal. They find the lens of feminism to be distorting, ideological, and political. Consider what it signals for Rush Limbaugh to call some women "feminazis," or the implications of conservative pundits' blaming feminists for America's vulnerability as revealed in the attacks of September 11, 2001.

The lens metaphor can make it sound as though gender is just one special interest among many. The metaphor suggests a gender lens will help analysts perceive and remedy male dominance. By extension, the lens metaphor also suggests a race lens will help analysts perceive and remedy white supremacy and a class lens will help analysts perceive and remedy capitalism. But in none of these cases does remedy follow directly from perception. Moreover, race, class, and gender are not so easily separated. The experiences and writings of working-class women, women of color, and women and men who do not conform to heteronormative standards suggest that masculinity and femininity are internally differentiated in ways that have much to do with race, class, sexuality, and nationality. The gender lens metaphor can seem too unitary for understanding the complex and contradictory realities of difference and dominance. The metaphor of overlapping lenses (of gender, race, class, nation, and sexuality, for example) or of faceted lenses (that reveal multiple, simultaneous social inequalities) can become cumbersome.

Finally, the gender lens metaphor can present a falsely monolithic notion of feminists, feminisms, and feminist theories. The metaphor of a gender lens can make it hard to present and discuss the conceptual, methodological, theoretical, and political distinctions among feminists. Reasonable people—many of whom it might be important to consider or include as 'feminists'—disagree on the evidence and arguments involved in studying gender relations, states and social policies, and how they affect each other. In chapters 3 and 4, I make a special effort to include some of the diversity among feminist researchers. In the two concluding chapters, I speak directly to the problems I perceive in what have become the dominant ways of studying gender, states, and social policies. For a more technical discussion that draws on a wider range of scholarship, is not constrained by the gender lens metaphor, and is less tightly focused on the United States, see my article on this subject in the journal *Social Politics* (Brush 2002).

In the next chapter I elaborate on the definition of gender I find most useful in studying states and social policies. And throughout this book, when I use the lens metaphor for gender, it is generally as a very preliminary critique, in the corrective sense. I try to complicate it with attention to variation and to both historical and local specificity (still with a focus on the welfare states that are the apparatus of rule in capitalist democracies, and with particular reference to liberalism and the United States). In addition, throughout the text I draw on examples at varying intersections of privilege and inequality, including gender.

Without the corrective offered by a gender lens, the assertion that gender power and state power are mutually constitutive seems counterintuitive. Many political theories—the intellectual tools people use to explain states, social policies, and political processes—are androcentric. That is, they assume a masculine point of view but call it universalism or neutrality. Pluralists view the state as a neutral arbiter among a variety of similarly situated competing interests, and ignore male dominance as a force in politics. Marxists view the state as a site and force for the consolidation and contestation of class power. They assume the key interests of capitalist states are neutral with respect to gender. Power elite theorists similarly claim that a coherent ruling class dominates corporations, governments, and policy networks. They sometimes neglect to mention that the vast majority of owners, winners, and decision makers in business, government, and the media are presumptively heterosexual men of the dominant ethnic group. Democratic theorists seem to forget that unless women are half of the decision makers and leaders, the 'people' of *demos* is masculine, not universal. They are just beginning to grapple with the paradox that expansions of democracy (or at least of the franchise) around the world were frequently accompanied by explicit exclusions of women. Discourse theorists appear not to notice that their intermittent attention to masculinity and femininity as a system of signs and meanings relegates gender to an often-belittled realm of culture and symbol.

As the contradictory and contentious issues about privacy I raised earlier illustrate, liberalism is especially blind to its own gendered character. Distinguishing between public and private is neither natural nor always good for women. In fact, making the liberal distinction between state and civil society, public and private, is a gendered political practice. Feminist political philosophers as diverse as Wendy Brown (1988, 1995), Zillah Eisenstein (1993), Jean Bethke Elshtain (1995), Catharine MacKinnon (1989), and Carole Pateman (1988) observe that traditional liberal ideology excludes many people from full political personhood and participation, and consigns women and other subordinate groups to languish in private. Liberalism establishes criteria for political participation (such as freedom, integrity, autonomy, and reason) that are antonyms for proper femininity. As a consequence, women in liberal political systems have to rely on markets, families, or specifically feminist struggle rather than conventional politics to address issues of gendered inequality, exploitation, violence, and domination. Women in other political systems rely on religious or military authorities, party officials, or male family members to present their claims or protect their interests. Or women may have enhanced access to the apparatus of rule through the feminist bureaucrats Hester Eisenstein (1996) called "femocrats," through formal and informal links between the women's movement and state institutions, or through a division, department, or bureau of 'women's affairs' (see chapters 3 and 4 and the references therein).

Without the corrective of a gender lens, the evidence and effects of male dominance in politics are invisible—exactly the way the pattern in a polarized windshield is invisible until you look at it through the polarized lenses of your Ray-Ban sunglasses. Masculinity is the unexamined foundation of norms of leadership, government, and politics. A gender lens reveals the masculine bias of politics as usual. To see the gender of politics is to perceive the ways men and masculinity are considered simultaneously normative, prescriptive, and objective in the definitions of, for example, free and equal persons and their rights and duties. To see gender in states and social policies is to observe the ways women and femininity are rendered simultaneously deviant, unruly, and subordinate. And to perceive gender in states and social policies is to note the ways political practices and rhetoric make male dominance and female subordination seem natural, universal, and inevitable.

I show in this book that gender happens in the rules of law, the administration of citizenship benefits, the definitions of expertise and activism, and the mobilization of political power to designate and address social problems. States and social policies set criteria for proper manliness and acceptable femininity. They reproduce gender difference and dominance in both their internal organization and their expectations about citizens and politicians and their duties and capacities. States, in short, are one place 'where the power is' in specifically gendered terms. If feminists want to organize effectively against male dominance, being able to perceive gender power in states and social policies offers an important strategic advantage over gender blindness.

Two decades ago, the masculinist assumptions she observed in states and social policies prompted feminist legal and political theorist Catharine MacKinnon to wonder, "What is this state, from women's point of view?"

What, in gender terms, are the state's norms of accountability, sources of power, real constituency? Is the state to some degree autonomous of the interests of men or an integral expression of them? Does the state embody and serve male interests in its form, dynamics, relation to society, and specific policies? Is the state constructed upon the subordination of women? If so, how does male power become state power? . . . Is masculinity inherent in the state form as such, or is some other form of state, or some other way of governing, distinguishable or imaginable? (1983, pp. 643–644)

MacKinnon's questions sound abstract. The notion of ascertaining (let alone generalizing about) "male interests," "male power," "masculinity," or "men's welfare" seems quaint if not bizarre. However, the stakes are high. States are at least one notable place 'where the power is' in contemporary societies. State power and its exercise have implications for men, women, and relations between us.

At their best, the powers and programs of the state can offer women leverage against masculine privilege in bed, at home, on the job, at school, and on the street. Laws and social policies can make it easier for women to speak up, fight back, and take charge. The entitlements and benefits of citizenship can promote women's economic welfare, full personhood, and participation in the common life. Political mandates and public policies can materially and morally undermine the material, institutional, and cultural bases of gender segregation, discrimination, exploitation, and domination. As Ann Crittenden (2001) shows, for example, reforms can ease the costs to women as we experiment with new intimate relationships, work arrangements, and notions of citizenship. Political processes offer the potential for women's participation alongside men in deliberation, legislation, administration, and self-governance. Most radical of all, from a feminist point of view, women's meaningful political participation potentially changes not just the distribution but the definition and deployment of economic, social, and political power.

This feminist sense of radical political possibility is utopian. I do not mean 'utopian' as a condemnatory epithet. Rather, it is a descriptive measure of the distance between how far feminists have come and the distance yet to be traveled. Visible changes in the conditions of women and other oppressed groups matter immensely in everyday life, and can in-

spire feminist insurrection. But visible changes can also "mask the permanence of . . . invisible structures" that reproduce masculine domination
(Bourdieu 2001, p. 106). After all, the broader dream of equality, freedom,
accountability, peace, and shared responsibility is just as utopian as the
feminist sense of political possibility. Feminists should not give up on
either set of possibilities just because we are unlikely to see them fully
realized in our lifetimes.

Feminist efforts to change states and social policies in a wide variety
of countries have won significant improvements for women. In many
countries, especially the capitalist welfare states that are the main focus
of this book, women have made great strides in educational and employment opportunity, equal pay, citizenship rights and benefits, political participation and representation, health care (including access to abortion
and prenatal care), child care, and campaigns against workplace sexual
harassment, rape, and other violence against women. Some scholars
argue that these improvements in women's lives are the result of feminist
activists building coalitions, winning concessions, and changing political
institutions, capacities, and ideologies (see e.g., Mazur 2001; Stetson
2001). Others argue that increased gender egalitarianism is instead the
product of gender-neutral rationalization and the drive for profit and efficiency in modern capitalist firms and state bureaucracies (see e.g., Jackson 1998). Either way, these empirical examples constitute best-case
scenarios for feminist engagements with the power of states and social
policies.

In contrast, at their worst the powers of the state can reinforce patterns of disadvantage and privilege. Social policies shape attitudes, outcomes, and incentives for change. In liberal welfare states, policies and
practices of foreign trade, foreign aid, and immigration, for example, and
the regulation, surveillance, and sometimes force required to implement
them, all shape women's and men's lives. Fundamentalist theocracies
condemn women to seclusion, subordination, starvation, and worse. In
fascist states, social order rests on a deeply gendered moral order that
gives pride of place to physical strength and discipline (Bock 1983; Bourdieu 2001). Policies and their implementation can place women and men
in impossible dilemmas over fairly sharing life's dangers, joys, and bur-
dens. Putatively gender-blind legal systems literally take the standpoint
of the "reasonable man" and thus trivialize or run roughshod over
women's lives, needs, and injuries. Elected officials create policies that
compel women into unwanted motherhood, or authorize forcible sterili-

zation of women who have had children they 'cannot afford.' Welfare reforms designed to reinforce marriage can trap women in poverty and in dangerous economic, emotional, and practical dependencies on hostile or indifferent men.

As feminist state theorist Wendy Brown rightly points out, appeals to the state for rights, recognition, or protection are at least as likely to "produce regulated, subordinated, and disciplined state subjects" as they are to generate informed, justice-seeking, rebellious political activists (1995, p. 173). However, the possibility of suboptimal outcomes should inspire rather than deter feminist efforts to analyze and challenge states and social policies. I address this point at greater length in the final chapter. But at the very least, recognizing the potential negative effects of state power on men, women, and gender relations—and wanting to make change—motivates feminists' understanding states and social policies.

In this book, I use a gender lens to contribute to feminist understandings of how male dominance organizes states and social policies. A gender lens allows assessment of the different effects state power and social policies have on men and women. A gender lens reveals the role of policy in the social construction of both difference and dominance. A gender lens also shows the degree to which masculinity, femininity, male dominance, and female subordination organize state power, institutions, personnel, procedures, policies, and rhetoric. By viewing states and social policies through a gender lens, this book aims to ask and answer questions that will both develop feminist descriptions of how state power produces inequality, and analyze state power as a gendered hierarchy. Throughout this book, but especially in the two middle chapters, I gather evidence to answer two questions.

➢ To what extent and how do states and social policies regulate, mandate, or ameliorate gendered social organization at home, on the job, in communities, and between sexual partners? Answering this question involves analyzing what I call the *governance of gender*, that is, the ways states and social policies set the rules and circumstances under which we become women and men and accept or reject the different and unequal life chances assigned to us.

➢ To what extent and how are state power, institutions, and policies organized around femininity and masculinity, male dominance and female subordination? Answering this question involves investigating what I call the *gender of governance*, that is, the variable degree to which assumptions about masculinity and femininity, male privilege and female penalty, structure the logic, determine the personnel, influence the budget, and otherwise organize the institutions and practices of states and social policies.

I use a gender lens to view structures, procedures, and discourses as well as results of governance. Looking at states and social policies through a gender lens shows the gender of governance and its effects on the governance of gender. A gender lens also reveals the extent to which truths we hold to be self-evident sometimes rest uneasily on women's subordination.

The Organization of This Book

The book is organized into three sections. In chapter 2, the other introductory chapter, I elaborate what I mean by *governance* and *gender*. I compare theories of power, viewing them through a gender lens, and introduce various ways of thinking about states and social policies. I also set out in some detail the notion of gender I use. Chapter 2 covers an enormous amount of ground, and ranges across a wide set of ideas in the political and social sciences, setting the foundation for what comes later in the book. The basic message of the chapter concerns the close links between notions of power, on the one hand, and notions of governance and gender, on the other hand.

In the middle two chapters, I build a more empirical argument about the usefulness of a gender lens for analyzing states and social policies. Focusing tightly on welfare states in the North Atlantic, and particularly the United States, I use a range of historical examples to elaborate the principles from the first section and document the governance of gender and then the gender of governance, the two facets of a gender lens on state power and social policies. In chapter 3, I assess the ways states and social policies not only *regard* and *reward* but also *produce* and *position* women and men as different and unequal. In chapter 4, I look at the ways gender organizes states and social policies in terms of representation and in terms of major structural features of governance such as the gendered division between public and private, the gendered origin myths of classical liberal political theory, and the "two-tiered" character of the welfare state. I distinguish between an analysis rooted in *women in government* and an analysis rooted in the *gender of governance*. Throughout, I refer whenever possible to what researchers and activists have learned about gender and governance specifically by attending to issues of violence against women.

In the last section of the book, I explore some of the implications of understanding the governance of gender and the gender of governance, and of including violence against women in feminist accounts of states and social policies. In chapter 5, I suggest that using a gender lens to understand states and social policies requires changing the subject of gendered welfare state studies. Instead of focusing so intently on *working mothers*—the privileged subject of both scholarship and politics—I propose that the proper political subject of feminist scholarship and activism is *women in movement*—women acting alone and in concert to struggle for our own and more general emancipation.

Finally, in chapter 6, I engage the lively debates between optimistic and pessimistic assessments of the state as a terrain for feminist action. Yes, feminists run the risk of increasing conventional power when we engage in struggles to reform the state. Yes, some historical struggles for women's rights mobilized racist and xenophobic sentiments, or justified women's political activism in terms of moral purity that merely reiterated gendered divisions of labor, rights, and duties. But empirical evidence from numerous cases and my analysis of the governance of gender and the gender of governance also suggests there are multiple points of contradiction and possibilities for struggle. If feminists take a hint from Willie Sutton and see states and social policies as "where the power is," we can make a difference in the quality of people's lives. We can also change the rules and tools available to the next generation.

CHAPTER 2

Governance and Gender

Consider the difference between *governor* and *governess*. The difference maps the gendered contours of distinctions at the heart of social and political life. Common sense and scholarship alike distinguish between public and private, political and personal, legislature and nursery. No one mistakes the hand that guides the ship of state for the hand that rocks the cradle. No one would have called Ella Grasso, the Connecticut politician who was the first woman in U.S. history to serve as the independently elected chief executive of a state government, "Governess Grasso."

Attending meaningfully to the difference between *governor* and *governess*—and its consequences for governance and gender—is possible if we use a gender lens to view states and social policies. In this chapter, I focus on defining *governance* and *gender*. I explain my choices among the many available ways of defining and analyzing both states and gender. I argue that how analysts think about power and gender shapes notions of governance, and that viewing states and social policies through a gender lens requires some conceptual retooling. To start, I discuss two different ways of thinking about what I mean by 'power' when I claim that *states are where the power is*.

What Is Power?

There is little consensus among social and political theorists on the meanings and sources of power. Definitions reveal and conceal aspects of social life. They reinforce or contradict the interests of particular analysts and social groups. In addition, reaching consensus on defining power is hard at least in part because definitions of abstract phenomena such as power, energy, work, or love tend to be metaphorical. Choice of metaphor is never innocent. Nor is the point of metaphor, definition, or analysis merely to convey meaning. The point, in social science at least, is to convince everyone that *your* metaphor best corresponds to the referent, or best characterizes the facts, and will consequently be most useful in understanding and shaping events.

In a socially differentiated world, what you see and how you interpret it depends on where you are, where you look, and who wants to know. The roads and terrain of Gaza map differently for refugees, foreign tourists, state-sponsored settlers, delivery truck or ambulance drivers, and soldiers. Boundaries, intersections, housing developments, olive groves, and checkpoints have different meanings—and constitute different types of locations—for different observers and actors. Moreover, those different meanings are not arbitrary or random. They depend systematically on who you are, where you are from, what you are doing, and whether someone is supporting or shooting at you. Not surprisingly, different metaphors, definitions, and mappings of power reflect and privilege different positions in systems of power relations. Similarly, where and who you are determine what you see when you look at power and the state.

It is important to keep in mind these problems of definition as I set out and then use a gender lens to inspect two of the many ways of defining and understanding power, one from Max Weber (1978) and the other from Michael Foucault (1977; 1980). I inspect these two notions of power with particular care in part because they are especially influential. But my account also shows that, in terms of the requirements of a theory of power sufficient to the task of understanding states and social policies as 'where the power is,' Weberian and Foucauldian models have complementary strengths and weaknesses. Together, they are a good place to begin.

The writings of political sociologist Max Weber provide the definition of power most familiar in the social sciences. For Weberians, power is the ability to act willfully even against the resistance of others. Weber distinguished among economic, communal, and political power, and posited social honor, material life conditions, and authority as sources of social power (Wright 2002). However, Weber's definition implicitly assumed that force or coercion is the ultimate source of power. This is not exactly 'might makes right,' which would be the case if we always equated the strong with the good. But it is definitely 'force trumps,' in which case the pen is mightier than the sword only when journalists also carry semiautomatic weapons.

Classically Weberian power is *power over*. That is, power is the ability to get things done your way even when someone tries to thwart you. According to such a model, you can tell who has power by noting who benefits—economically, politically, socially, and personally—from current arrangements. Who reaps rewards and who gets ripped off? Who runs the place and who has no say? Who limits debate and who can't even get on the agenda? Who wins disputes or elections and who is a spoiler or a perpetual 'also ran'? These empirical questions make visible the traces or results of Weberian *power over*. New Age negotiation manuals and arbitration models that emphasize 'getting to yes' or 'win-win solutions' are *not* based on Weberian models of power.

Power in the Weberian model is analogous to energy in Newtonian physics, and follows the equivalent of the laws of thermodynamics. Given a closed system, power is neither created nor destroyed; it merely changes form. Change requires investment to overcome inertia. Without investment, the course of events will tend to follow the path of least resistance, and power will disperse. Moreover, power in the Weberian model is zero-sum. Again given a closed system, if one person or group gains power, others lose. The typical Weberian metaphors for power are militaristic (the fist, the jackboot) or commercial (whoever pays the piper calls the tune). Weber's own most famous metaphor is industrial and mechanical. According to Weber, the Protestant ethic of delayed gratification and demonstration of salvation through material acquisition turned accumulation into the juggernaut of capitalist economic development. Those same values become a trap in which subsequent generations find themselves trudging ever faster on a treadmill not of their own making—caught in an "iron cage" (1998, p. 181).

An alternate line of reasoning is associated with French social theorist Michel Foucault (1988). According to Foucault, power and the contests that generate, maintain, and resist it (that is, politics) permeate the entire social order. In Foucault's model, the same practices of power that provide individuals with private modes of conduct also provide public information and social control. In contrast to Weber, Foucault presented power as a set of institutions and procedures that increase rather than repress potential conflict. Power in a Foucauldian model contains disruptive instabilities by multiplying sites for regulation.

Rather than force or money, *knowledge* is fundamental for Foucault. His central metaphors are organic, linguistic, and architectural. Power for Foucault is *capillary*, that is, dispersed, pervasive, and interactive, instead of concentrated, centralized, and top-down. For Foucault, power is also *disciplinary*, that is, based on routine compliance and conformity to expert criteria. Disciplinary routines, once internalized, become habitual. And for Foucault, power/knowledge is *discursive*, that is, constituted in practices of speech, vocabularies of image and classification, and struggles over meaning.

The haunting metaphor, at least from the early Foucault (1977), is not the iron cage but the eye in the door. Foucault gives pride of place to the *panopticon*, an innovation in prison architecture and management that partially transferred the responsibility of maintaining discipline from guards to inmates. Knowing that they may be observed at any moment by a single guard at the visual center of a ring of cells constantly open to inspection, inmates internalize the watchful gaze of the guard and regulate their own behavior. Spectacular punishments such as public execution, flogging, and the stocks give way in modern times to intimately intrusive surveillance tactics such as deathbed confession, census forms, and psychological tests. Power changes accordingly. State power in particular is rooted less in brute force and war and more in keeping track of and disciplining everyday conduct. In a Foucauldian model, the modern state is less a warfare state, with power literally embodied in the hereditary monarch—*L'état, c'est moi*—and increasingly a bureaucratically administered welfare state (1988; 1991). Power is dispersed through civil servants, experts, and the clients from whom they attempt to coax both information (that is, the knowledge that is the basis for expert power) and right conduct.

Unlike the overwhelming force of a Weberian model, Foucault observes that as the sites of power and knowledge proliferate, so do the possibilities for resistance. Power is in the relationships between experts and clients, for example. Although sheer force may not render resistance futile, resistance is a problem in a Foucauldian model. Attempts to counter disciplinary power, Foucault argues, often merely augment and legitimate the forces of surveillance and expertise by assuming and drawing attention to them. For Foucault, when you 'fight the power' you give it energy and augment its strength, if only by perpetuating the idea that there is something worth fighting.

In weighing Weberian and Foucauldian notions of power and the foundations they each provide for building theories of states and social policies, it is especially important to keep in mind the strengths and weaknesses of Foucault's emphasis on power as discursive and disciplinary. Yes, knowledge and meanings are important. Signs, symbols, meanings, and speech are all elements of power. Efforts to control the creation and circulation of oppositional ideas and independent thought are a hallmark of totalitarian political power. This is vividly illustrated by the climactic scene in George Orwell's dystopic novel *1984*, in which the Thought Police undermine an ordinary citizen's capacity for independence and rebellion by persuading him that "2 + 2 = 5." Winston Smith betrays his lover, Julia, and capitulates to the power of Big Brother by agreeing to the counterintuitive nonsense of this equation.

Orwell's protagonist stands for both the importance and the fragility of individuality, independence, and thought in politics. Indeed, this dynamic of totalitarian control through torture that exploits the tight links among empirical observation, independent thought, empathy, and capacity for rebellion has become a cultural fixture. Consider the homage to Orwell in Captain Jean-Luc Picard's interrogation and torture by the imperialist Cardassians in an episode of *Star Trek: The Next Generation*. The setting of Picard's ordeal is centuries and light-years distant from "Room 101" where Winston Smith came to know that "He loved Big Brother" (1948, p. 245). But the situation and the importance of 2 + 2 = 5 are the same, as is the point about power and knowledge. These examples of thought control in representations of totalitarianism from popular culture suggest the importance of Foucault's notion of power. Theorizing power—even state power—as not just bureaucratic and military but symbolic and discursive helps social and political scientists think about aspects of states and social policies (for instance, culture and language) that are outside the purview of Weber's model.

However, signs and symbols are clearly not the only forms or sources of power. Capitalism, states and social policies, white supremacy, imperialism, and male dominance are unlikely to be canceled due to lack of interest. They will not wither away simply because people refuse to pay attention to them. Contemporary states are simultaneously militaristic and bureaucratic, institutions and ideologies, distant and intrusive, hierarchical and capillary, deeds and words. States command social workers, garbage collectors, and public librarians in addition to lawyers, guns, and money. As political scientist Wendy Brown (1995) points out, contemporary welfare states have liberal, capitalist, militarist, and bureaucratic dimensions or modalities. States and social policies rely on no single source or mode of power. State power, institutions, and procedures are complicated. Reducing complicated power relations to a single dimension (such as force or knowledge) is likely to result in misleading oversimplification. Mistakenly exaggerating the importance of one aspect over another will inspire poor political strategies.

The point is that different notions of power obscure and reveal different ways in which states and social policies might be privileged sites or modes for social change. Where you look determines what you see. The degree to which state power appears 'gender neutral' or not depends in large part on whether observers focus on territory, taxes, welfare benefits, or zoning laws, and on whether the notion of power that analysts privilege emphasizes force of arms or ideas. Thus, the complexity of states and social policies recommends drawing insights from wherever they are available, even if that means models of power as different as those of Weber and Foucault.

Weber and Foucault through a Gender Lens

Viewed through a gender lens, neither Weberian nor Foucauldian definitions of power fully capture the features required for a feminist theory of states and social policies. Weber's definition has all the problems of liberalism. For instance, Weber takes for granted the division between public and private, political and personal. The division is gendered but invisible. That is, Weber's notion of power privileges masculinity while it simultaneously considers the distinction between public and private to be neutral and normative. Although he questions the distinction between state and civil society, Foucault's definition is also gender blind and therefore masculinist. To see the gender of power, feminist political philosopher Nancy Hartsock notes (1983), we have only to remark on the ways power is commonly associated with *domination* and *virility*— qualities intimately linked to masculinity since at least the ancient Greek philosophers. In particular, many feminists distinguish between 'power over' (referred to in the discussion of Weber above) and 'power to.' 'Power over' is about domination. 'Power to' is about empowerment. 'Power over' is revealed in the ability to overcome resistance. 'Power to' is revealed in the ability to call upon, articulate, and coordinate the abilities of others in order to accomplish tasks or achieve common goals.

Hartsock and other feminists associate the Weberian notion of 'power over' with masculinity. Weberian notions of power emphasize force, territory, competition, repression, and domination, quite traditionally masculine concerns. Through a gender lens, it is relatively easy to see the gender of power in the case of Weber. Foucault, on the other hand, eschews repression and domination as the most interesting modes and metaphors of power. After all, what is masculine about power conceived as capillary?! Hartsock analyzes the cultural value of virility. Her explanation of the notion of power as *eros* exposes the gendered qualities of models that conceive power as commanding submission and denying or repressing sensuality. Hartsock and other feminist philosophers, such as Nancy Fraser (1989) and Marilyn Frye (1983), reveal the extent to which Foucault ignores the gendered dimensions of power, resistance, discipline, and expertise. After all, if knowledge is power, and women are by definition not knowing subjects, Foucault would appear to have missed the important fact that the power to know is gendered. If power and knowledge are disciplinary, and women are forever considered the mysterious unknown (to be prodded, queried, measured, and constructed, ironically, through means Foucault would find familiar even though he did not explore them in terms of gender), there are important gendered practices and meanings of power/knowledge invisible to Foucault's scrutiny.

Here is what is lacking in these two widely used notions of power: Neither Weber nor Foucault addresses the power to destroy dignity and integrity and to deny personhood through sexual violation. This is a central concern of feminist politics. Neither notes private tyranny and men's power derived from the ability to shame, starve, torture, beat, or rape women into submission. This has been a central concern of feminists organizing against battering, prostituting, or trafficking in women, some of which efforts have been directed toward states and social policies. It has been up to feminists such as Susan Bordo (1991) and Kirsten Dellinger and Christine Williams (1997) to test a 'docile body hypothesis' with studies of gendered practices of makeup, exercise, and disordered eating. None of this occurred to Foucault, although he theorized the docile body as one produced and disciplined through power/knowledge.

In one Weberian definition, the state is the institution within a territory with a monopoly of legitimate force. What do we do with the fact that men's violence against women at home has often been normative, legitimate, and legal? Is a man's home therefore a state? Weber cannot imagine, let alone answer, this question. As Frances Restuccia (2000) points out in the case of battered women, Joy James (1996) notes in the case of racist lynchings, and the crucifixion of gay martyr Matthew Shepard on a fence in Wyoming so vividly illustrate, 'spectacular punishment' for embodied, racialized, gendered, and queer subjects is far from over. Foucault misses elements of state power, sexism, racism, and heterosexual privilege that turn 'surveillance' and 'discipline' back into state-sanctioned spectacles of wounded, dead, and dismembered bodies. Moreover, neither Weber nor Foucault can accommodate the power of creativity or of nurturing the capacities of others, the power to move or stir or coordinate not against resistance but in concert ('power to'). All these alternative notions of power are part of the feminist critique Hartsock presents, drawing on diverse feminist influences such as Hannah Arendt (1951) and Hannah Pitkin (1967).

Even Weber's concept of charisma, a kind of personal force of command and leadership, is more about 'power over' than 'power to,' and thus seems masculinist. Foucault seems to have room for desire as power, but he is in the end less interested in desire than in discipline. Moreover, the myriad and profoundly human ways experience or art can move us—to laughter, to tears, to pity, to action—are entirely outside the realm of both Weberian and Foucauldian definitions of power. Hartsock usefully summarizes the ways different women theorize power and politics to include precisely this meaning. When viewed through a gender lens, Weberian and Foucauldian notions of power leave vast areas of social life unexplored. By omission, they trivialize women's experience. Weber and even Foucault (with all his focus on sexuality) therefore offer limited guidance in understanding the gender dynamics and ramifications of the sexual double standard for, say, welfare policy.

Foucault risks missing the forest for the trees, or perhaps misses the clenched fist because he is so fascinated by capillaries. Besides, Weber is at least as aware as Foucault of the importance of bureaucratic and other noneconomic modes of power. But Foucault (and Marx before him) argues persuasively that power is a relationship, not a pie to be distributed in zero-sum slices. Moreover, *power over* is distinct from *power to*. When I assert *states are where the power is*, I am at least partially adopting Weber's contention that force is often the source of power to which people turn as a last resort. But satisfactory notions of power, even of something as institutional and structural and violent as state power, have to include other dimensions. The outcomes of most power struggles are complicated and hard to attribute to a single cause. Better to treat it as an empirical question whether and when money, force, cunning, technology, or love triumphs.

Power in States and Social Policies

Power matters because power is so obviously and centrally what states are about. There are as many notions of state power as there are general political theories. State power may be the will and ability of the Prince to maintain sovereignty over his principality using whatever brutal means seem necessary, as the realist Machiavelli (1977) advised. State power may derive from civil society, where free and equal citizens consent to establish a more perfect union and thus provide for the general welfare, as the classical liberals such as John Locke (1952) claim. State power ultimately may rest in a monopoly of force and legitimate authority, as Weber (1978) would have it. Or state power may reside in the ability of the dominant economic class to appoint an executive committee to rule on its own behalf, as Marx and Engels assert in their *Communist Manifesto* (1970). Then again, state power may circulate through the technologies of surveillance and resistance, population statistics, public health, and policing, as Foucault proposes (1988, 1991). State power may rest in the collective capacities of people to assess and meet their own needs, cooperate, and transform their common life, as some democratic theorists insist. State power may institutionalize and legitimate men's domination and control of women, fertility, and sexuality, as some feminists argue. Or state power may offer women a means of organizing against private tyranny, political exclusion, corporate discrimination, and violence, as other feminists contend.

For my purposes, what is important to note is that different approaches to defining and analyzing states and social policies go along with different concepts of power. Furthermore, different notions of power and concomitant approaches to states and social policies have far-reaching ramifications for how analysts think about gender and politics. A quick review of the links among power, states, and gender in a number of traditions of political theory will both orient the reader and simultaneously drive home what I mean when I assert *states are where the power is*.

Pluralists claim that states facilitate collective actions and recognize preexisting collective identities of existing social groups jousting on the proverbial level playing field. If pluralists think about gender at all, they view women and men as two of many competing lobbies or special interest groups, whose identities and desires are set before the players step into the political realm. *Utilitarians* and other *rational choice theorists* emphasize how strategic actors assess the costs and benefits of competing ends and means. Some rational choice theorists, like pluralists, treat personnel and processes of government as neutral with respect to gender. Others view the gendered component of politics as driven by competitive, evolutionary, or other 'natural,' amoral forces that only incidentally result in domination or inequality. Still others see the incentives for rationality and efficiency characteristic of capitalism, bureaucracy, and electoral politics as gradually but inevitably eroding masculine privilege.

Functionalists assess the degree to which particular state administrative practices or policies serve social needs for order and intergenerational continuity. *Conflict theorists* determine the extent to which particular policies or institutional arrangements serve contested organizational, class, race, or gender interests—for example, in Helga Hernes's (1987) terms, the extent to which the state is "friendly" to women.

As do pluralists and utilitarians, *instrumentalists* view the state as neutral. They claim that the gendered character of the state rests on the fact that the closer you get to the pinnacle of power, the more likely the incumbents are men. Men are therefore able to use the state as a set of tools to further masculinist ends. The assumption follows that if only more women were elected and appointed to positions within the state, we could similarly wield state power in our own interests. *Structuralists*, in contrast, claim that the gendered character of the state comes from the disparate impact of gender-blind or outright discriminatory decision rules and principled decisions about, say, the appropriate role states play in regulating markets and families. Structuralists hold that what matters is not just who controls the toolbox of the state, but whether it features primarily Phillips head or regular screwdrivers, metric or imperial measures, or electric drills and a jackhammer.

Finally, *poststructuralists* show how politicians, bureaucrats, and other experts selectively define citizenship and constitute state subjects through talk about identity, normality, rights, needs, recognition, and redistribution. Poststructuralists view power as a decentralized, fragmented way to use discursive resources to contest and make meaning. When they recognize the gendered character of discursive practices in general and expertise in particular, poststructuralists incorporate gender power into their accounts of state-building and its consequences.

There is also as much variation in *feminist* theories of the state as there is among feminist theories generally. Feminist state theories share the notion that gender relations are socially constructed and therefore subject to political contest and historical change. Feminist state theories generally acknowledge the complex and interconnected character of gender, race, and class. Most feminists agree that states and social policies have important effects on oppression, and that oppressive power relations shape institutions, capacities, and ideologies *within* states and relations *between* them.

However, some feminist theories are instrumentalist, some structuralist, some poststructuralist, and others pluralist or liberal in the senses set out above. In addition, feminist state theories differ in the relative weights they assign to the importance of various factors in assessing state interventions in women's status and everyday experiences. Some stress employment, others family life, while still others emphasize citizenship, law, welfare policies, and social service practices, or global contexts of conquest and exploitation, symbolic representation, or violence against women. Feminists vary widely in their degree of optimism about the opportunities states present for radical transformation or even modest reform and amelioration of gendered social relations.

To a certain extent, the variations in feminist state theories are artifacts of using alternative facets of a gender lens to look at states and social policies. Different researchers and activists look at diverse institutions, capacities, and ideologies of assorted states at distinct points in time, so it is small wonder that they perceive somewhat different patterns. However, some variations in feminist state theories are related to political and material differences among feminists. As noted above, there are important distinctions among realist, utilitarian, pluralist, and Weberian-versus-Foucauldian notions of state power. It should not be surprising that there also are tensions and controversies among the priorities, approaches, and assessments of radical lesbian, liberal, and social-democratic feminists from various parts of the world.

This book is not intended to adjudicate among the multitude of approaches to power, states, and theory. Instead, I assume that each approach draws attention to a specific aspect of state power, and what matters is where (and of course that!) you pay attention. Various aspects of state power and institutions have implications for understanding the gender of governance and the governance of gender. In this book, I focus on the theoretical and historical origins of welfare states, state institutional organization and law, personnel, and mobilization. A multidimensional approach encourages looking at different parts of the state and diverse dynamics of governance. A multidimensional approach also encourages looking at different aspects and measures of gender, for example, the proportion of men or the sexist assumptions that characterize different state bureaucracies at different points in time. I use the conceptual distinction at the heart of this book—between how *states govern gender* and how *gender organizes governance*—to structure my multidimensional inspection of states and social policies through a gender lens.

Government, Governance, Governmentality, and Gender

Political scientists define *government* as "the agencies of highest public authority for a particular territorial unit . . . continuous across particular administrations . . . [and] act[ing] through but . . . not identical to political institutions or administrative structures" (Weldon 2002). *Governance*, for mainstream political science, is "the process of implementing modern state power, of putting the program of those who govern into place" (Duerst-Lahti & Kelly 1995, p. 12). These definitions are adequate for my purposes, at least insofar as I talk specifically about states and social policies. However, gender is often not explicit but rather implicit in the program of those who govern and the agencies of highest public authority. I therefore want to introduce a somewhat broader and more sociologically imaginative concept of governance. I draw here from Foucault's (1988; 1991) lectures on the political technology of individuals and on what he calls *governmentality*. Because (as I noted above) Foucault routinely ignores gender, however, I modify his insights on power and knowledge with reference to Canadian feminist theorist and institutional ethnographer Dorothy Smith's (1987) work on gender in the social relations of ruling.

For Foucault, governing means much more than it means in conventional politics. Recall that Foucault's notion of power is capillary, disciplinary, and discursive. Governing the self requires disciplines of personal conduct or morality plus regimes of personal care (hygiene, exercise, dress and cosmetics, comportment, posture, accented speech). Governing souls requires pastoral doctrine, liturgy, ritual, sermonic and homiletic composition, and confession. Governing children requires pedagogy, juvenile 'justice' and detention systems, and child psychology. Governing a family requires economy, meticulous accounting, and control of the means of maintaining inheritance and reputation. Governing the state requires statistics assessing the size, well-being, and capacities of the population. Power in these activities of governance is dispersed and intimate, based on knowledge gleaned through surveillance, and results in proliferating speech and habitual conformity enforced by expertise.

According to Foucault, governance happens everywhere. Consequently, in every realm of modern life, governance constructs certain subject locations and subjectivities, specific states of mind. This *governmentality*—the mentality and power/knowledge behind governing selves—is a broader meaning I invoke with the term *governance*. The concept of governmentality implies that state power is intimately involved in constructing expert knowledge, official power, and the conditions of everyday life by surveying populations.

To govern requires detailed knowledge of the strength and capacity of the state, including not only its territory but also its people. Population dynamics, productive capacity, and public health are therefore central state concerns. The capacity to assess population is for Foucault a key form of modern political power. States account for the strengths and weaknesses of population through political arithmetic. For Foucault, political arithmetic extends beyond figuring out who is with you and who against you by counting votes. Political arithmetic means assessing the strength of the state by developing reliable knowledge of the human resources—and influence over the conduct—of the nation-state. What counts in Foucauldian political arithmetic are people and their parts: able hands, fertile wombs, healthy babies. Accounting is a form of governance. It is intimate and intrusive, even when carried out by a Census Bureau official or welfare administrator instead of a pastor, paternalistic employer, or head of a family.

Thus Foucault sees governance as extending beyond the formal state apparatus to professional expertise, business management, and social scientific and information control more generally. For the most part I will focus on conventional aspects of governance, such as elections, policies, and institutions that are recognizably part of the bureaucratic state. However, Foucault usefully insists that building the state conventionally defined has also been about establishing and bolstering certain professions. States historically depend on professionals and their clients, which means that state building is about experts and their prestige, their revenue base, their turf. Therefore, sometimes my discussions of the governance of gender and the gender of governance will invoke broader notions of rule, for example professional disciplines that may overlap but are not necessarily coterminous with official state bureaucrats. For the most part, I will refer to social workers, who have a particular professional relationship to states and social policies throughout their history (mostly since the 1880s) in the United States. But what I have to say about governance, gender, and the links between professional and official/state disciplines sometimes also includes lawyers, demographers, juvenile court judges and probation officers, urban planners and public administrators, and public health nurses.

Foucault, for all his concern with deeply gendered phenomena of health, fertility, population, expertise, labor, and sexuality, ignores the gendered character of governance and governmentality. He blithely reproduces the assumption that citizens, workers, professionals, princes, paupers, and state officials are somehow universal. In fact they are often gendered, that is, polarized into masculine or feminine, with the masculine privileged and the feminine subordinated. Just as Weber never questions the male monopoly on legitimate force, Foucault never questions the specific consequences of male monopolies of expertise or state power. Similarly, Foucault ignores the gendered fact that maintaining inheritance and reputation in a male dominant society requires men's control of women's fertility and sexuality and that governance is therefore gendered (see, for example, works by historian Gerda Lerner [1986] or political theorists such as Catharine MacKinnon [1989] or Jacqueline Stevens [1999]).

In sharp contrast, institutional ethnographer Dorothy Smith (1987) specifically uses the concept of governance in her feminist epistemological argument. Viewing the world from the perspective of women, it is impossible to miss the gendered character of expert knowledge and the relations of ruling it makes possible. Smith shows that the abstract mentality of governance rests on the taken-for-granted concrete world. That taken-for-granted world is in fact maintained by hard work (Bourdieu 2001 embroiders this point). Managers, government officials, and experts seldom acknowledge the invisible labor on which governance rests. Part of the reason the labor that makes possible abstract thought and governmentality is invisible is because much of it is performed by underpaid women. Women are often deemed insufficiently objective, abstract, or disinterested to govern themselves or discipline children, let alone rule society. States, social policies, expertise, and the mentality of government are gendered to the core. *Fundamentally, this book seeks to substantiate Smith's assertion, and to explore what looking at governance through a gender lens tells us about how and why gender relations are built into the apparatus of rule.* In that same pioneering essay, in which she directed us to look at the state and law from women's point of view, MacKinnon made a key distinction. "Feminism has descriptions of the state's treatment of the gender difference," MacKinnon said, "but no analysis of the state as gender hierarchy" (1983, p. 643). What she meant is that feminists have produced lots of theory and evidence about the differential treatment of women and men in law and policy and politics. Feminists have amply documented the resulting inequalities in economic well-being, political representation, and other outcomes in everyday life. Feminists have also assessed the effects of women's social movements and political action on institutions, capacities, and ideologies and therefore on the limits and possibilities of women's lives. However, feminists have only begun to explore the gendered organization of state institutions.

Previous scholarship on gender, states, and social policies has documented and asked hard questions about the origins, maintenance, and possible futures of governments that produce unequal outcomes for women and men. But showing unequal outcomes does not exhaustively explain the gendered character of the state. And assessing the differences between women and men as policy makers, political candidates, or bureaucrats only scratches the surface of the ways and reasons states seem to view and treat women the way men view and treat women (MacKinnon 1989).

Therefore, this book also looks at states and social policies through a gender lens by analyzing the gendering of governance, that is, the gendered organization of state institutions and policy practices. I present evidence that not just the outcomes but the procedures and structures of states are gendered. By using a gender lens to view the *structures, procedures*, and *discourses* as well as the *results* of governance, this book contributes to state theory and helps develop gender as a concept in political and structural analysis.

The Gender in 'Gender Lens'

Contemporary feminist social scientists locate gender in interactions and institutions as well as individuals. In their handbook of social science research, for instance, sociologists Myra Marx Ferree and Beth Hess collected research and theory to support their assertion that gender "is not a trait but a system for dividing people . . . [It is] relational rather than essential, structural rather than individual" (1987, pp. 16–17). Gender, in short, is not something people acquire or even perform, let alone a trait that they have. It is far more than that.

People are assigned their places in (and seek to defend or disrupt) the gender order because gender is a central mechanism of *social recognition*. That is, gender is a basic classificatory scheme. Gender establishes a supposedly straightforward, intuitively and physically obvious, and putatively universal difference as the basis for meaning, in the cognitive as well as the semantic sense. From this blunt yet meaningful classification scheme flow rank, power, privilege, and the perpetuation of women's subordination across vastly different material conditions and situations (Ridgeway 1997; Johnson 1997). Much of what human beings do requires that we acknowledge and attend to one another. Therefore, mechanisms of social recognition—the means by which we classify others as similar to ourselves (or not) and therefore having equal or legitimate claims (or not)—are fundamental to organizing interactions and institutions. Thinking of gender as a mechanism of social recognition thus places gender at the center of social organization at the level of interaction and institution.

Thinking of gender institutionally stands in sharp contrast to perhaps more familiar role theories of gender. The concept of role has two main applications in social science, one *dramaturgical* and the other *structural*. Dramaturgical models are based in a metaphor of society as theater, complete with actors, scripts, and stage directions. In dramaturgical models, scripted, reciprocal rituals of interaction and recognition define situations, organize social life, and limit both people's actions and the outcomes of social processes. Structural models are based in a metaphor of society as architecture, complete with foundations and glass ceilings. In structural models, where you are relative to others and to centers of resources or power sets the limits and possibilities of what you do and feel, and who you and others consider you to be.

Gender roles in the dramaturgical sense refer to the notion that masculinity and femininity are repertoires of communicative action used by actors and audiences. The central metaphor is that of actor and script. In this model, people 'do' gender (on this notion in particular, see West & Zimmerman 1987 and West & Fenstermaker 1995). Interactions and their settings (front stage and back stage) are the social locales of interest. Face-to-face interactions construct the self, and microlevel interactions incrementally and iteratively construct macrostructures. Audience responses give social actors feedback (including positive and negative sanctions). Audience feedback helps social actors conduct themselves in accordance with social expectations, a central element in ordering the potential chaos of everyday interactions. Learning how to 'act like a lady' or 'take it like a man' are typical examples.

One of the most completely realized feminist versions of dramaturgical gender role theory is to be found in Judith Butler's 1990 book, *Gender Trouble*. Butler conceptualized gender as *performance*. Butler focused particular attention on the example of drag, in which people—through cross-dressing and otherwise affecting traits and postures stereotypically associated with masculine or feminine roles—playfully take on exaggerated attributes of gender roles at odds with the category to which they have been assigned. Thus, men performing as drag queens affect an over-the-top presentation of femininity, for instance as 'diva,' which they 'do' in many respects more convincingly than any women other than professional performers such as Diana Ross or Celine Dion. (Women also perform masculinity in drag, for example, Madonna or k. d. lang appearing in a 'man-tailored' suit, or burlesque performer Shelly Mars, who plays the sexist Australian egomaniac Martin in a baggy suit and mustache.) Butler argues that the fact that men can perform femininity and women can perform masculinity contradicts the natural status and 'given' character of gender. For Butler, the playful, flexible, deliberate, and frequently outrageous practices of drag (and camp) exemplify the fact that gender is socially constructed and a matter of performance. In her 1993 book *Bodies that Matter: On the Discursive Limits of 'Sex'*, Butler renounced the voluntaristic aspects of gendered role theory. Gender is not something we take on or off at will. Butler's revision recognized the extent to which gender attributes endure because of the profound extent to which they reproduce social relations and conditions of domination in people's bodies and psyches. Butler's notion of gender as socially structured performance stretches the feminist usefulness of dramaturgical role theory to its limit.

In the structural sense, roles are sets of behaviors and attitudes associated with specific positions or locations in society. Each role is associated with a functional position, and its complement is associated with a functional counterposition. Position and counterposition are like two sides of an interactional coin—boss and worker, teller and bank robber, john and prostitute, for example. The status and actions appropriate to the role are given by the position, its location in social space, and the function the position and counterposition are supposed to fulfill. The self preexists, and roles may be ascribed (the role of 'adolescent') or achieved (the role of 'professor'). Whether roles are given by circumstances and life course or accomplished by dint of hard work, macrostructures constrain micro-level processes, and expectations and sanctions create and enforce social order.

In both the dramaturgical and structural senses, actions and attitudes are specific to the role and independent of the person who fills it. In some dramaturgical models, the face may grow to fit the mask, and accomplished social actors commonly slip so easily and comfortably into their roles that they surpass the greatest artists of stage and screen. Still, as in structural models, the person is different from the position, even though position, practice, and posture may sharply constrain possibility. Moreover, in both dramaturgical and structural role theories, masculinity and femininity are generally (although not without historical and cultural exception) complementary, mutually exclusive, and exhaustive categories. That is, heterosexuality is assumed and you may normally be a man or a woman but not both, neither, or something else. In both the dramaturgical and structural versions, the content of the roles of masculinity and femininity and the assignment of specific persons or types of persons to their roles is understood to be given by nature. The pairing of husband and wife is the quintessential example.

Sociologists R. W. Connell (1987) and Allen Johnson (1997) provide particularly astute assessments of role theory for understanding gender (see also the classic 1985 essay by sociologists Judith Stacey and Barrie Thorne, the 1987 critique of Talcott Parsons by Evelyn Nakano Glenn, and Helen Lopata's 1983 essay on 'women's roles'). Connell and Johnson are both careful to point out that whether structural or dramaturgical, role theories are attractive for feminist purposes because they metaphorically confirm the fundamentally social character of gender difference, male dominance, and women's subordination. Role theories shift the emphasis in explaining social phenomena from 'nature' to 'nurture.' They connect individual life experiences and personality to anonymous social structures. Role theories create a vocabulary for social interaction, especially role conflicts of various types. Through the distinction between the person and the role, role theories emphasize the social processes of gender acquisition. They thus offer hope for more egalitarian ways of raising children and eventually organizing social life. Also through the distinction between the person and the role, role theories make it possible to criticize some aspects of behavior and social relations without condemning the incumbent of the position or the person behind the mask. Role theories hold out the promise that acting against stereotypes, for instance, is an effective means of changing society. For some, including Butler, the metaphor of role and script also draws important attention to the notion of play in gender—both in the sense of flexibility and in the sense of disrupting the status quo by not taking it quite so seriously.

Unfortunately, the greatest strength of role theories as a way of conceptualizing gender—the emphasis on the social by talking about expectations and interaction—hides three traps. One is the voluntarism trap. Role theories claim that people take their signals from the sanctions applied to role performance. Individuals respond to rewards for conformity and punishments for departures from the norm. But why do people apply sanctions to enforce roles? This quickly degenerates into a chicken-and-egg problem of expectations ("I expected you to expect me to expect you . . ."). The assumption of voluntarism—that is, the claim that people enforce roles because they choose to maintain existing customs—is especially a problem in talking about gender, in part because it means people tend to blame inequality on tradition without talking about power (Allen Johnson is eloquent on this point; voluntarism is the trap Judith Butler takes particular care to escape in her more recent work).

The second trap is essentialism. Gender roles are unique among role theories to the extent that biological categories (some essential femininity and masculinity that evolved, along with opposable thumbs, bipedal locomotion, and the capacity for speech, over the course of primate development) actually determine these supposedly social roles. This is especially true of the structuralist variants of sex role theory, rooted as they are in functional counterpositions: what other than natural selection could define the 'role' of mother as lactating caregiver? As with the voluntarism trap, the political effect is to highlight the informal pressures that create an artificially rigid distinction between women and men. Essentialism plays down the economic, domestic, and political power that men exercise over women. Contemporary social scientists seldom speak of race roles or class roles. True, race and gender are both categories with contested biological bases, and eugenic justifications for racism and class elitism persist. However, biological essentialism remains respectable as the intuitive basis for sexism, while biological racism is generally shunned in polite company. Similarly, the rich might not be like the rest of us, but if the rich are different, it is due more to monetary than to genetic inheritance. The exercise of power in race relations and class conflict is much more obvious than in the case of men and women, where the roles are treated as complementary.

Complementarity is a trap because, as Allen Johnson points out, 'man' and 'woman' are not functional counterpositions in the same sense as teacher and pupil or pimp and trick. Masculinity and femininity appear to have meaning only as mutually exclusive, exhaustive, and naturally complementary categories. However, the assumption embedded in role theory that masculinity and femininity are complementary (which naturalizes not just gender relations but also heterosexuality) is just that: a political assumption. The strict dichotomization or polarization of masculinity and femininity is likewise socially and politically constructed, variable, and contested. In part because of these three traps, role theory is far from the last word in gender.

In contrast, feminist social psychologist Sandra Bem proposes a way of thinking about gender that I find useful for exploring the governance of gender and the gendering of governance. Bem introduces her concept of gender this way:

> Throughout the history of Western culture, three beliefs about women and men have prevailed: that they have fundamentally different psychological and sexual natures [gender polarization], that men are inherently the dominant or superior sex [androcentrism], and that both male-female difference and male dominance are natural [biological essentialism]. (1993, p. 1)

These three assumptions, "embedded in cultural discourses, social institutions, and individual psyches, . . . invisibly and systematically reproduce male power in generation after generation" (p. 2). Bem calls gender polarization, androcentrism, and biological essentialism the "lenses of gender." She analyzes how they "shape how people perceive, conceive, and discuss social reality" *and* "systematically reproduce male power" because "the discourses and social institutions in which they are embedded automatically channel females and males into different and unequal life situations" (pp. 2–3). Bem provides a model for thinking about how complex organizations and the social interactions and individual outcomes they regulate are gendered: precisely to the extent and in the ways that they manifest and reproduce androcentrism, gender polarization, and biological essentialism.

There is nothing new about Bem's three concepts. Critiques of androcentrism in particular have a distinguished legacy in feminist theory, and the concept is central to longstanding feminist analyses of everything from legal method and objectivist epistemology to popular culture. Feminists have long recognized the ways deliberate or unintended ambiguity, historical and cross-cultural variation, and the human capacity for play and flexibility undermine purely polarized notions of gender. Evolutionary psychology is just the most recent reiteration of a form of biological essentialism that maintains masculine privilege and reproduces and aggravates male-female differences by naturalizing them. But Bem's model pulls these three concepts together as linked mechanisms, straightforwardly described. Bem also shares with the Gender Lens series a sense of the fruitfulness of the "lens" metaphor. I would add that particular institutional and policy arrangements *vary* in the degree to which they bolster or undermine gender polarization, androcentrism, and biological essentialism. They also vary in the extent to which the three lenses reinforce or contradict one another in the same site and at the same time. I refer to the concepts of gender polarization, androcentrism, and biological essentialism throughout the rest of this book.

To sum up: Gender is not something you *are*. Despite the deeply subjective experience of masculinity and femininity, the profoundly embodied character of the desires and feelings that organize gendered personhood, and the sometimes personal, intimate character of gender power, it is not you. Certainly, gender is not *all* you are. The lives and writings of women of color, working-class women, women living in exile or diaspora, and lesbians, for example, draw attention to the ways 'who we are' include race-ethnicity, class, nation, and sexuality as well as gender.

Gender is not something you *have*. Designation is not the same as possession. At birth or before, you are assigned to a gender category. Gender assignment is established and maintained by people in authority (such as doctors or court clerks) operating in an official capacity for the state (e.g., filling out a birth certificate or marriage license). In terms of race as well as gender, birth records and marriage licenses constitute important forms of power/knowledge for political arithmetic. People take gender (and race) classification and conformity seriously from the very beginning, and throughout the life course. In some rare cultures, people get to choose gender later. In those not-as-rare-as-you'd-think cases of ambiguity, gender assignment may be accompanied by surgery, hormone treatments, and doggedly determined efforts at heteronormative socialization. Properly socialized people acquire the skills and knowledge required competently to interpret and enact their designated gender. Moreover, people who wish to 'pass' as members of the other gender—like people of color tempted or encouraged to 'pass' as white—can learn how to enact the appropriate postures, gestures, and speech patterns. This is one salutary lesson to draw from Judith Butler's notion of "performativity." However, gender is not just a story of socialization into conformity. Gender is not only the acquisition of a set of presumably appropriate traits.

Gender is not just *women*. Gender is both women and men, both femininity and masculinity. It is also the relations between them and all the people and practices that do not fit neatly into these dichotomized categories. Gender is, moreover, the social relations that construct masculinity and femininity as exhaustive and mutually exclusive categories, that see men and the masculine as universal and normative and cast women and the feminine as peripheral or deviant, and that portray anatomy as destiny. Gender is the romanticized notion that masculinity and femininity are inherently complementary. The eroticization of gender complementarity is at the root of the myth that heterosexuality is natural and inevitable or in some meaningful sense chosen freely in the context of male supremacy and hostility to women's autonomous sexuality in general and lesbianism in particular.

Gender is something you *do*, although it is also more than that. The gender regimen—for example, the body disciplines of working out, dieting, or putting on makeup, the postural disciplines of walking, talking, dressing, and gesturing like a lady or a real man (or dealing with the confusing and sometimes dangerous consequences if you do not)—is enforced and enacted both in solitude and in small and large groups, and is fundamentally interactive. You get to be a competent, acceptable, or rebellious woman or man through practice and habitual response to feedback from other people. Gender is also done differently, depending on race-ethnicity, class, sexuality, and nation—further evidence of the social, historical character of gender.

Gender also has nothing to do with you, so do not take it personally! Gender is one way of organizing social life, from the intimate desires of individuals to the mass markets of the economy to the vast bureaucracies of corporations and governments. Gender is a *place* in social relations. Gender positioning consistently results in women's individual and collective sexual, political, economic, and social subordination. The positional character of gender is sufficiently obvious that it leads intuitively to a personalistic solipsism. That is, people often assume that women can upend gender relations by getting their individual selves into positions of relative power and control. Thus the slogan with which Smith College undergraduates commemorated their school centennial: a sexualized double entendre celebrating "a century of women on top." Unfortunately, women who reach powerful positions in commerce or government frequently do so at the expense of the familial and especially maternal connections that define them as 'fulfilled' women. This persistent conflict gives the lie to the personalistic solipsism. So does the fact that "to say of a woman in a position of power that she is 'very feminine' is just a particularly subtle way of denying her the right to the specifically masculine attribute of power" (Bourdieu 2001, pp. 99, 107). Male dominance is not so simply reversed. However, it *is* about men and women, masculinity and femininity, in unequal relation to one another. Gender regulates positions in the social order. Gender and male dominance persist in part because they organize control, fear, and aggressive competition in predictable ways (again, Allen Johnson makes this point with exceptional clarity). Gender is a way of representing and reproducing power relations—not only between women and men, but more generally (in her 1988 book, historian Joan Wallach Scott says this as persuasively as anyone in feminist scholarship).

Gender is not synonymous with *feminism*. Gender is a concept for understanding the social creation and relations of masculinity and femininity. Feminism is most simply the politics of women's insubordination. Feminism is the antidote to the invisibility of women (and gender power) created by the false claims to universalism of masculinism (what Bem would call androcentrism). To the extent that the concept of gender is useful to the politics of women's liberation, feminism and gender overlap. But analyses that give gender pride of place, and the politics that flow from them, may or may not be feminist. The gap between gender and feminism is likely to be large when studies of gender focus on particular aspects typical of many women's lives (say, motherhood or family life or caregiving) without emphasizing the fact that they are conditions of subordination or suspect power. Not all social movements or collective actions of women are feminist (see, e.g., Blee 1998). Class, race, sexuality, and nation shape not only the experiences of women and men but also feminist politics. Moreover, feminists sometimes worry that 'gender' is just another way of smuggling men back to the center of analysis. I share some of these anxieties about the substitution of 'gender' for feminism. I hope in this book to recognize and join the feminist scholars of gender, critics of masculine privilege *and* women's subordination, who analyze gender power in order to promote women's emancipation.

Gender produces masculinity and femininity, women and men. This implies that the category of 'woman'—the foundation not just of scholarly analysis but of individual identity and collective mobilization—is not a *given*, it is a *construct*. As French feminist philosopher Simone de Beauvoir (1961) famously put it, women are made, not born. Gender analysis, especially in its more postmodern and discursive forms, seeks to understand the practices that constitute feminine (and masculine) subjects and give different meanings to 'woman' (and 'man') in various social contexts.

Gender is a *principle of social organization*. Through gender, people organize individual subjectivity and make meaning from the barrage of data we sort moment to moment. Through gender, people organize the human life course. Gender starts in the womb; consider the technologies that allow selective abortion of female fetuses to realize the preference for male children that persist in many cultures (Rothman 1989). Gender lasts to the tomb; gravestone epitaphs reveal gendered relationships and priorities (Martineau 1988). People use gender to organize face-to-face interaction. People use gender to organize groups small and large, from dyads to corporations, their internal dynamics, and their encounters with other groups. People use gender to organize social institutions—small, intimate institutions such as families, and also huge, impersonal ones such as law, religion, the economy, and, I argue in this book, states and social policies. Gendered logic informs the places where women and men encounter one another, and also designates places that are sometimes thought of as 'separate spheres'—the world of work and politics for men, the family and home for women. People use gender to organize the apparent divisions between home and work, private and public, state and civil society. In addition, the gendered organization of social life varies from one place to another, changes over time, and differs by class, race-ethnicity, and other dimensions of stratification.

Although male dominance includes efforts to control women's bodies, fertility, and sexuality, gender does not just happen in families, and gender organizes more than kinship, reproduction, and inheritance. Gender is not based in some primal division of power over life and death, in which femininity is exclusively maternal while masculinity is by default associated with killing (partly because paternity is so uncertain). Families, factories, battlefields, banks (and bank robbers!), and even such puta-tively universal concepts, processes, and institutions as patriotism, power, imperialism, deindustrialization, and globalization are organized so that they are consistent with androcentrism, gender polarization, and biologi-cal essentialism. Gender happens everywhere, although to varying de-grees and different effects.

Gender is *hard work*—and it is also hard work to hide the social labor of gender, so that gender appears natural and beyond question. The key idea to keep in mind when thinking about gender as individual, interac-tive, and institutional is this: The levels of social organization where peo-ple do the hard work of gender and perceive the results are mutually reinforcing. The work of gendering produces individual dispositions, feelings, responses, ambitions, and interactions that reflect and fit with what everyone observes everyday in broader social organization, such as the division of labor or the separation of public and private. This corre-spondence between subjective experience and institutional organization, between individual development and social structure, makes our gen-dered traits and desires feel intuitive, and renders gendered social struc-tures invisible and resilient in the face of feminist critique and reform efforts. Catharine MacKinnon refers to this correspondence when she says, "Women's situation offers no outside to stand on or gaze at, no inside to escape to, too much urgency to wait, no place else to go, and nothing to use but the twisted tools that have been shoved down our throats" (1983, p. 639). The work of gendering also produces institutions that reward and punish according to gendered conformity criteria that reflect and fit with androcentric principles that everyone perceives as uni-versal, such as competition, distinction, and domination. The fit between structure and subjectivity makes the gendered organization of institu-tions seem natural, and erases the social labor that goes into gender. Pierre Bourdieu (2001) echoes Catharine MacKinnon (1987), Gayle Rubin (1975), and many other feminists when he points to the way this corre-spondence between individuals and institutions hides "the endlessly re-commenced historical labor which is necessary in order to wrench masculine domination from history and from the historical mechanisms and actions which are responsible for its apparent dehistoricization" (p. 103).

Everything is gendered, but gender isn't everything. As I have sug-gested by hinting at the variation in gender as experience and organizing principle for poor women, women of color, and lesbians, complex societies and subjectivities are organized and stratified by other principles, too, including most prominently but not exclusively class and race-ethnicity. Like gender, race-ethnicity and class are not merely traits we have but what we do and how we do it and the social relations and contexts that give meaning to and set limits on our doing. Along with gender, race-ethnicity and class also organize our personal feelings, sense of identity, and repertoires of speech and gesture. Along with gender, class and race-ethnicity also organize the division of labor, the rewards of work, the risks and benefits of sexual adventuresomeness, crime and punishment, hunger and homelessness, and the heartache of a dream deferred. Like gender, race-ethnicity and class have historically determined what scientists and chroniclers in every era and discipline perceive and proclaim as Truth. Race-ethnicity, class, nation, and sexuality shape the experiences and consequences of gender. Gender shapes the experiences and consequences of race-ethnicity, class, sexuality, and nation. By using a gender lens, this book highlights how gender practices and locations matter for understanding states and social policies—while attending to other important dimensions of power and the variations they produce in gendered lives and organization.

PART 2

Governance through a Gender Lens

CHAPTER 3

The Governance of Gender

The argument that states govern gender rests in the end on evidence gathered to answer a number of empirical questions. Do states and social policies turn girls into women and boys into men? Do they contribute to the compulsory distinction between girls and boys, women and men? Do they privilege some men and forms of masculinity at the expense of most women and notions of femininity? Or, in the term R. W. Connell introduced in his 1995 book, do states and social policies reinforce or undermine "hegemonic masculinity"? Do they rely on and reinforce the 'naturalness' of gender difference and male superiority, in accordance with God's law or Darwin's? Do they contribute to creating gendered civilians and soldiers, elected and appointed officials, social workers and welfare recipients, cops and bank robbers, johns, pimps, and prostitutes? In other words, do political institutions and practices generate and reinforce gender polarization, androcentrism, and biological essentialism?

The short answer to these questions is "Yes." Both the questions and answer come into particularly sharp focus when viewing states and social policies through a gender lens. States and social policies are like other complex organizations and social processes. The institutions and practices of governance produce gender difference and male dominance as they mark meaning, establish and contest terrain (geographic, economic, or intellectual and professional), and otherwise organize power in collective life. Moreover, the short answer obtains even without resorting to examples from seemingly anomalous, anachronistic, or exotic 'rogue states' that, in the twenty-first century, deny women suffrage, sequester women and girls, mandate men's control of women's travel and social contacts, and enforce gender polarization and androcentrism with corporeal and even capital punishment.

The longer answer, and the aim of this chapter, involves understanding the ways in which states and social policies not only *regard* and *reward,* but also *position* and *produce* masculinity and femininity, and thus govern gender. To use a gender lens to inspect states and social policies and therefore to perceive how they govern gender involves looking at the gendered outcomes or results of the exercise of state power (in terms of both *regarding* and *rewarding* citizen-subjects), and at the creation and regulation, construction and instruction, of proper women and men (whom they both *produce* and *position*). This differential regarding and rewarding, producing and positioning of men and women is what I mean by the *governance of gender.*

Women and men contribute to proper notions and practices of masculinity and femininity as they resist or conform in their everyday lives. Historian Linda Gordon reminded feminists trying to think about states and welfare that institutions, policies, and practices result from struggle. Important political contests take place "not only between organized political forces but also between individuals" such as social workers and clients, public health nurses and patients, and juvenile court judges and 'delinquents' (1990, p. 5). Evidence of the governance of gender involves both the processes and practices that structure people's agency. So: How do the various institutions and practices of governance shape people's opportunities, resources, and everyday experiences? What are the gendered effects and consequences of governance? How do states and social policies distinguish governors from governesses, and ensure that individuals of the appropriate gender wind up in the 'right' social locations, knowing how to behave? These are the questions that motivate this chapter.

Three Possibilities for the Governance of Gender

The claim that states and social policies *govern gender* suggests at least three possibilities simultaneously. One, states govern already-gendered persons, and are therefore neutral terrain or referees. Two, states govern through formerly sexist but increasingly reformed or 'modernized' rules and institutions, leading to the incremental, inevitable decline in gender inequality. Three, states produce, position, regard, and reward women and men in ways that vary over time, across nations, and among groups (by race-ethnicity, sexuality, and position in what Immanuel Wallerstein in 1974 called the "world-system," for example). Each is a different sort of claim, supported by different evidence. However, they are not mutually exclusive. In fact, the third of these suggestions incorporates important elements of the first two, and comes closest to what I mean when I assert that states govern gender. In this chapter, therefore, I focus empirically on evidence of states' governing gender by producing, positioning, regarding, and rewarding women and men. However, I also present the arguments and some of the evidence associated with the first two approaches. Attending to the contrast among these arguments helps to substantiate my case for favoring one approach as empirically, theoretically, and politically most compelling, innovative, and suited to the feminist task of viewing states and social policies through a gender lens.

First, the notion that states govern gender suggests that gendered citizen-subjects encounter fundamentally neutral or neuter state institutions, personnel, and practices. This suggestion is a variation on a pluralist model of power, states, and social policies. Recall from the previous chapter that according to pluralist models, states facilitate collective actions and recognize preexisting collective identities of already-constituted social groups jousting on the proverbial level playing field. Gender-blind states face preestablished gender differences and gendered citizen-subjects. The claim is not so much that *states and social policies are gendered*, or that they *govern gender*, as it is that *states govern gendered societies*.

According to this argument, women and men have different leadership styles, policy concerns and priorities, political cultures, organizational networks, and modes of mobilization. Those differences could be natural, the results of evolved biological predispositions. From this point of view, the evolutionary imperatives of survival push men to develop qualities of competition, conquest, and command and women to develop complementary qualities of domesticity, peace, and nurturance. Or the differences between women and men, and women's subordination, could be social and historical. In this way of looking at gender differences and dominance, they result from actions, choices, and preferences. They are structured by expectations, opportunities, and struggle rather than by hormones, upper-body strength, and natural selection.

Either way—nature or nurture—women and men experience different treatment and outcomes when they run for office, lobby for policy, claim benefits, seek protection, compete for government contracts, join the military, call for or run from the cops, or otherwise bump up against state institutions. According to this model, differences in treatment and outcome result because when they encounter welfare workers, electoral procedures, members of Congress, cops, or the armed forces, citizens are *already constituted as women and men.* People are already divided into masculine and feminine. At one level, this is obviously true. Therefore, the differences they experience when they encounter states and social policies are not caused by their being divided or distinguished by the mechanisms, institutions, or practices of governance. In this way of thinking about it, states and social policies govern gender only to the extent that they serve as neutral referees.

Arguments that treat governing gender as a matter of states as neutral referee tend to measure the gendered effects of governance in terms of women's relative political weakness. Evidence of that weakness consists of women's vast underrepresentation among elected, appointed, and inherited officials in most countries throughout history. Further evidence comes from women's dismal records of policy influence and political accomplishment even after achieving suffrage. Historically, women in most capitalist democracies have had small political influence limited to 'marginal' issues such as drunk driving or maternal and child welfare—as opposed to 'central' questions of national security, foreign trade, or fiscal policy, where women have less impact. This evidence substantiates a feminist critique of women's relative political weakness. An element of the governance of gender is visible in the differences between women's and men's political power (and, as I argue in the next chapter, in differences between women's and men's presence 'where the power is').

At best, these models account for women's limited political accomplishments with reference to the shifting influence of policy networks, ideological climates, or electoral strategies such as bloc voting. Political sociologist Theda Skocpol (1992), for example, attributed the rapid spread of state-level cash assistance programs for poor mothers and their children in the United States during the 1910s (known as Mother's Aid) to women's activist organizations, a popular discourse of child protection, and state legislatures susceptible to pressure from both. In contrast to the moral bankruptcy of the patronage-based Civil War pension system, Mothers' Aid legislation had an organized and credible constituency able to argue that at least some poor mothers (limited for the most part to white, native-born, hardworking, celibate widows) deserved protections parallel to those previously offered soldiers, veterans, and their survivors.

Historian Robyn Muncy (1991) similarly traced the rise and fall of a "female dominion in American reform" prior to the New Deal as a function of shifting organizational opportunities, institutional arrangements, and gendered professional competition. Men won because they commanded greater power and resources. However, women put up a good fight, facilitated by inclusion (e.g., in the franchise in 1920) and motivated by exclusion (e.g., from many sectors of the academy and other professions during the Progressive Era; see also the 1990 collective biography of four U.S. women reformers of this period by historian Ellen Fitzpatrick). In these accounts and others like them (see for instance those on a variety of countries collected by Seth Koven and Sonya Michel 1993), social policies that support maternal and child welfare, regularize military pensions, and otherwise regulate gender relations or affect women and men differently result when *differently motivated, organized, and empowered women and men confront the same (basically neutral) institutions of governance.* This historical research documents and explains the differences in beliefs, priorities, resources, and strategies between the political movements, demands, organizations, and cultures of women and men. In their most feminist versions, such accounts also note the extensive effects of men's power and resources on the outcomes of political struggles.

At worst, models of the state as neutral referee attribute women's political weakness to gender, which generally implies that there is something wrong with women. According to such models, women fail politically because estrogen renders us too compassionate, too timid, or too distracted to compete in the dog-eat-dog world of politics. Men have more political clout than women because childhood socialization into proper femininity suppresses women's political ambitions and capacities for competition and self-promotion. Women's political weakness results from a feminine predilection for domesticity. Or women are underrepresented 'where the power is' due to 'choices,' as in an apparently natural and perfectly understandable preference for motherhood over equal pay or high heels over running for office.

According to this logic, there is a reason women could not vote in national elections in Switzerland until electoral reforms . . . in 1971. There is a reason no woman was elected to statewide office in New York before Hillary Rodham Clinton won her Senate seat . . . in 2000. There is a reason no woman served as assistant to the president for national security affairs prior to Condoleezza Rice's appointment by President George W. Bush . . . in 2001. There is a reason no woman rose to the rank of whip in the U.S. House of Representatives until Representative Nancy Pelosi became next in line to be speaker . . . in 2002. There is a reason political parties and parliaments around the world have to set quotas to fill their slates of candidates and seats in government with more than a token number of women, and even then often fail to be 'representative.'

According to this view, the reason women lag behind men in the political realm is not the power arrangements that preserve the androcentric status quo, such as the overwhelming odds that favor incumbents, or the fact that campaign organizers place women so far down on party lists that they stand no chance of election. The reason is not the popular assumption that the qualities of leadership are congruent with masculinity and therefore incompatible with femininity. The reason is not the fact that when men realize there is money or political power at stake in some particular realm of social policy (e.g., birth registration, infant mortality, and maternal and child health, in the cases Muncy and Skocpol explore; see also Cynthia Comacchio's 1993 book on the case of "baby saving" in Ontario, Canada), they have the resources and ability to muscle in even on policy areas that originated through women's organizing. The reason is not the historical context and economic imperatives of women's participation in politics. No, according to this logic, the reason is women's lack. Women lack skills, drive, charisma, and political savvy, all of which are symbolized by having a penis. As women lack this important piece of political equipment, being male still seems to be a key criterion for growing up to become president of the United States of America.

In terms of political strategies, the 'state as neutral referee' approach recommends women's changing to become more like the normative political actor, presumptively masculine. In this model, women enter politics through the aid of training and socialization or structural accommodations or affirmative action measures such as quotas. Such measures may indeed increase the competence and number of women in politics. However, they are designed to overcome differences between women and men that exist *outside* the state and *prior* to entering politics. That is not the only place gender happens, which is part of why such strategies will only ameliorate gendered political inequality to a limited degree. Such measures also require women's accepting androcentric political priorities and standards. African Americans such as Condoleezza Rice (George W. Bush's national security advisor) and Colin Powell (George W. Bush's secretary of state), and women such as Rice, Jean Kirkpatrick (Ronald Reagan's ambassador to the United Nations), and Madeleine Albright (Bill Clinton's secretary of state) sufficiently resembled the white men with corporate connections who served before them that they could be considered candidates eligible for traditionally male-dominated, racialized government appointments. Understanding the state as referee implies seeing states governing gender—and remedying inequality—by opening opportunities for participation to white women and to women and men of color *willing and able to act like white men*. Notions of the state as neutral referee fail to challenge this aspect of the androcentrism of states and social policies.

Pluralist models are unsatisfactory for feminist analyses of gender and governance partly because they blame women and partly because they ignore gendered features of political organization, states, and social policies. The claim is that women's relatively limited political power, the different treatment of mothers and soldiers as heroic figures of patriotic sacrifice, the preference for male doctors over female midwives as agents of public health, and other unequal outcomes when women and men encounter state practices, institutions, and policies, all come from preexisting differences between men and women. As difference is wrongly supposed to be the source of disadvantage, the strategy that pluralists propose for coping with the political ramifications of gender polarization in civil society—that is, encouraging women and other disenfranchised people to adopt the behaviors and attitudes of men—simply reproduces the masculine point of view as universal (androcentrism).

In the best cases, historians and other analysts attribute women's relative political weakness to women's failed strategies and limited power, combined with men's ability to assert, protect, and extend their interests. Analysts making this type of argument tend to assume that women fail and men succeed in politics due to factors that do not have much to do with the state itself. It is an important first step in analyzing the governance of gender to admit that masculinity and femininity are sources of difference and inequality in society at large. But notions of the state as level playing field or neutral referee lead to political strategies that reinforce androcentrism. Moreover, the 'referee hypothesis' discounts the possibility that political institutions and practices might create differences between women and men instead of just aggravate or compensate for them. Thus, it is not a very strong version of the argument that states and social policies actively govern gender.

In the second way of thinking about how states and social policies govern gender, current institutions and practices are gender neutral or very nearly so. They create identical incentives, opportunities, and dilemmas for all similarly situated political actors, or there is a strong trend in this direction. However, a legacy of historical disadvantage to women has consequences in the present for the differential success of women and men in political contests. According to such arguments, current political inequalities—between women and men, among racial-ethnic groups, or between the owning and working classes—are just historical remnants. Voting rights laws, redistricting, Supreme Court decisions, and campaign finance reform have supposedly rendered obsolete these systematic political disadvantages of race-ethnicity, gender, and class. Remaining differences between women and men are not caused by the gendered character of current arrangements but by the residue of the past.

Moreover, in this way of thinking, residual gender differences are unintended consequences. They are not the deliberate results of a patriarchal plot or men's ability to protect and extend their power and privilege at women's expense. On the contrary, residual gender differences are continually being eroded by "the migration of economic and political power outside households and its reorganization around business and political interests detached from gender [so that] . . . profit, political legitimacy, organizational stability, competitiveness, and similar considerations mattered more than male privileges vis-à-vis females" (Jackson 1998, pp. 2–3). The accelerating progress toward gender equality in politics in this model is the inevitable result of legal, administrative, and personnel changes requiring successful politicians, parties, and administrative regimes to replace antiquated male privileges with more efficient, modern gender egalitarianism.

In their most subtle and persuasive form, legacy arguments do not simply backdate the origins of inequality into the distant past. Nor do they assume that history is over, that is, that reformers have demanded and received every reasonable accommodation toward political gender equality. Persuasive versions of the legacy argument further deny that any remaining inequalities must result from natural or social attributes that differently suit women and men for political action, or to 'choice' (rationally calculated, 'free,' or otherwise). Instead, they emphasize the *combination and sequence of political developments in historical context*. It is the extent, order, context, and ongoing character of the processes in the development of modern governmental structures and procedures that determine the relative power of political actors and the capacities of states to govern and empower the people.

Legacy arguments can be empirically and theoretically compelling. Political scientist Martin Shefter (1977, 1978) persuasively argued that the relative power and capacities of different national governments, state administrative apparatuses, political parties, and interest groups depend on the order in which countries expanded the franchise, abolished patronage, established civil service bureaucracies, developed mass political parties, expanded industrial employment, legalized union organizing and collective bargaining, and the like. Strong, labor-oriented parties, entrenched systems of patronage, and civil service reforms as part of progressive and democratic movements result from different combinations of historical developments.

Shefter's work addressed a classic question: Why is there no strong labor party or democratic socialist electoral coalition in the United States? The question is gender blind, at least as Shefter and others generally pose and answer it. It is also race blind, to the extent that Shefter did not mention the ways slavery and racism created a North-South split that prevented working-class allegiance to a single political party (see research by Victoria Hattam 1993 or Richard Franklin Bensel 1990).

But when viewed through a gender lens, the question, the answer, and especially a historical sequences or legacies method and argument, generate some thought-provoking hypotheses. Historian Kathryn Kish Sklar (1993, 1995) argued that women's activism in the United States has often "done the work of class." In the United States, women have mobilized coalitions for economic and social justice and for progressive policy reform, to fight poverty, to improve working conditions, to regulate business, to protect consumers, and the like. They worked through systems of party, patronage, and philanthropy more friendly to women's activism than to (highly masculinized) class radicalism. This type of argument is different from arguments about the state as neutral referee that attribute women's differential political power and influence solely to characteristics or strategies of women. Sklar's model gives important explanatory weight to constellations of institutional and practical arrangements at particular historical moments. Theda Skocpol's (1992) comparative account of pensions for soldiers and mothers also features elements of this type of legacy argument. Because making policy is an iterative, recursive process, reform efforts at a given historical juncture have to take into account the results of previous successes or failures. Therefore, legacies are important. These historically specific, institutional accounts are the most compelling versions of the argument that *states govern gender through historic legacies.*

Political scientist Anna Harvey (1998) also made a legacy argument, but more from a rational-choice perspective. Recall from chapter 2 that rational-choice arguments typically emphasize the cost-benefit calculus actors use to assess and choose among ends-oriented strategies. Harvey argued that when U.S. women won the franchise, the prevailing constellation of institutional and organizational factors shaped women's subsequent political power and mobilization. The ways women organized to *win* the vote differed dramatically from the ways they needed to organize once women *had* the vote. Harvey explained women's subsequent failure to establish bloc voting as a feminist form of political mobilization and power in terms of this legacy.

From Harvey's perspective, it is not that women and men have different political cultures or predispositions, as claimed in the 'state as referee' model. Facing the same disadvantages and options, women and men behave equally rationally, and even pursue similar political goals, with similar results. Women won the franchise in the United States at a particular moment in the history of party mobilization and institutional development. The structural-institutional characteristics of that historical moment, not the gendered qualities of women and men as political actors or men's defense of their interests and privileges, explain women's relative political weakness. Women's exclusion from suffrage, Harvey argued, produced the same effects that men's exclusion would have, had masculinity per se been a criterion for exclusion from voting the same way femininity was. In Harvey's mind, the production of (hypothetical) identical effects for women and men means exclusion was not gendered.

This rational-choice approach is in many respects a significant advance over the pluralist understanding of gender as something peculiar to women. It is not that women have failed to secure equality and justice because of feminine notions of the appropriate degree of state intervention in civil society. Nor is the 'representation gap' due to gendered priorities, strategies for mobilization, or failure of political ambition. Nor is women's limited political leverage attributable to a temporarily chilly climate or backlash against feminist organizing.

After all, other groups besides women have faced similar hostility. Workers, immigrants, and disadvantaged racial-ethnic groups have all been excluded from the franchise at one time or another, in one place or another. Even after the passage of the Reconstruction Amendments, which rendered unconstitutional any racial-ethnic restrictions on men's voting in the United States, literacy tests, poll taxes, and violent intimidation were all used to deny voting rights to African Americans, whether they were born into slavery or not. That is part of why the question of irregularities in voter registration and ballot malfunctions in Florida in the 2000 Bush-Gore presidential election struck such a nerve—it appeared that both problems and demands for recounts systematically disadvantaged African American citizens.

Harvey conceded that *gender* has been a criterion of political exclusion, with effects similar to those of exclusions based on property, nativity, and race-ethnicity. Harvey contended that what matters is the fact of exclusion and the political facts of life at the point of inclusion, not the specific grounds for exclusion (which in this case was *femininity*). Thus, it was not women's political culture that resulted in women's limited collective political power after the passage of the Nineteenth Amendment, in 1920. Rather, women's organizations failed to change from the tactics required to *win* the vote to the tactics required to *use* the vote. It was a strategic mistake any group could have made—even men. When mainstream political parties stepped into the organizational breach, they precluded women's bloc voting *not because women were women* but because they were (generically) *poorly organized for partisan electoral politics*. Harvey's approach resolutely refuses to focus on, and to attribute meaningful causality to, the differences between women and men. Moreover, she unequivocally rejects appeals to male dominance as explanations for women's political disadvantage. In this respect, Harvey avoids the victim-blaming of many 'gendered political culture' and 'state as neutral referee' arguments.

The main problem with this type of argument, especially in Harvey's case, is that it fails to account for how specifically *gendered* politics and power are among the primary reasons that *femininity* has been a criterion relegating women to second-class citizenship. To put the problem the other way around, in terms of androcentrism, Harvey's legacy argument occludes the reasons that lack of masculinity has prevented women from conforming to the normative, putatively universal criteria for political participation. Masculinity and its historically variable stereotypical traits (aggressiveness, competitiveness, independence, decisiveness, and so on) have consistently been qualifying criteria for leadership, political clout, suffrage, and the like. Harvey cannot account for this fact nor understand why those criteria are the opposite of normal femininity.

Legacy models bring important aspects of history into the explanations of women's limited political power. However, if women's subordination is a consequence of rational choices, then why is male dominance so widespread, especially across quite different institutional arrangements and sets of political options? Without including some account of gender power, and the specificity of women's political exclusion and inclusion, purely rational-choice and legacy models of the governance of gender wind up begging the question.

The third notion suggested by the governance of gender is that states and social policies construct and instruct women and men in properly gendered identities, behaviors, expectations, opportunities, and realms of social life. The strongest version of the notion that states and social policies govern gender holds that political institutions and practices do far more than merely reflect or respond to gender polarization or androcentrism. Rather, states and social policies actively contribute to the maintenance of differences between women and men. They privilege men and masculinity, and subordinate women and femininity. The claim that states and social policies help set the criteria for acceptable masculinity and femininity further assumes that masculinity and femininity are not natural or preexisting categories, but social conditions. The notion that governmentality produces gender implies, moreover, that masculinity and femininity are lifetime accomplishments, not merely instruments—or relics—of childhood socialization. The notion of gender elaborated in the previous chapter is central here, especially the sense in which gender is not a trait but a power relation, constituted continually and interactively and circumscribed historically and socially, that people enact throughout their lives and deploy when they build institutions, exercise capacities, and create and perpetuate ideologies that make up the apparatus of rule.

The remainder of this chapter shows how states and social policies contribute to the governance of gender to the extent that they reinforce gender polarization by constructing and instructing women and men in contrasting ways. The evidence I marshal here also shows that states and social policies are androcentric to the extent that the governance of gender privileges men and masculinity, and disadvantages and devalues women and femininity. I also note how state actors, regulations, and organizational forms promulgate biological essentialism when they assume that the differences between women and men, and the privileges of masculinity and subordination of femininity, are natural. Patterns of exclusion and double standards reinforce gender polarization, androcentrism, and biological essentialism. The argument is that states and social policies not only regard and reward, but also produce and position femininity and masculinity and thus govern gender.

The following account of the ways states and social policies govern gender—which focuses primarily on the U.S. case—is intended to persuade readers of the existence of gendered effects of political life, and frequently uses examples of systematic disadvantage to women. However, the idea is not to present evidence of the governance of gender as a means of posing the state as everywhere, always, and in the same ways 'unfriendly' to women. Comparative research on gender and politics shows with particular clarity that the wide variety of political arrangements over time and geography results in a range of gendered effects. Readers interested in reading an extended appreciation and evaluation of the past decade of this research are referred to Anette Borchorst's 1999 review in the Gender Lens series collection *Revisioning Gender* or my 2002 article in *Social Politics*.

States, as the apparatus of rule in different countries, are characterized by a vast array of institutions, capacities, and ideologies. It is not surprising, therefore, that states vary in how, and the consistency with which, they govern gender. The governance of gender can include benefits, services, opportunities for participation, and other means of improving women's status and advancing feminist goals. A great deal of detailed policy analysis and comparative research (especially on welfare states in western Europe) shows that feminists' engagement with states and social policies can result in social change to ameliorate the conditions of women's everyday lives, remedy disparities in political representation, and otherwise reform gender relations. The governance of gender is not monolithic; it does not always regard and reward, produce and position women and men in the same way.

Indeed, Robert Max Jackson (1998) argued that gender inequality in politics (as in economics and other realms of life) is declining as the inevitable result of forces such as bureaucracy, economic efficiency, and mass electoral politics. Jackson posits these forces as gender neutral, as in fact constituting logics that make masculine domination increasingly inefficient and unsustainable over time. In contrast, the institutional conceptualization of gender discussed in chapter 2 perceives bureaucratic organization, efficiency, political mobilization, and other structural forces as gendered. *But whether states and social policies exaggerate or minimize differences between women and men, whether they reinforce or undermine male privilege, whether they aggravate or ameliorate women's subordination, they are in all cases governing gender.* The theoretical point holds whatever your political assessment of the usefulness or futility of feminist engagement with states and social policies.

The Politics of Exclusion from Politics

The most straightforward examples of the governance of gender clearly demonstrate sexist exclusion, bias, and discrimination. Gender (along with race, nativity, property, and sexuality) has been grounds for exclusion from the rights and obligations of first-class citizenship (such as suffrage and jury duty), and from civil, economic, and human rights. These exclusions have produced and positioned women and men as different and unequal members of the polity. They have regarded and rewarded women and men in gender-polarized, androcentric terms and naturalized women's exclusion.

A case in point is the fact that the U.S. Constitution did not explicitly distinguish between women and men until 1868. In the Fourteenth and Fifteenth Amendments (two-thirds of the Reconstruction Amendments referred to above), passed after the Civil War, full citizenship and voting rights were formally extended to men (including former slaves). Women were explicitly excluded from the groups whose rights received equal protection under the Reconstruction Amendments. The authors of the Reconstruction Amendments excluded women despite women's intensive organizing on their own behalf, despite women's contributions to the abolitionist movement, and despite women's occasionally craven willingness to mobilize racist, nativist, and elitist sentiments in the cause of female suffrage. It was another half-century before women won the franchise in national elections in the United States, not the first and far from the last country to grant women's suffrage equally with men's (for a compelling account of this constitutional history, see Reva Siegel 2002).

In 1848, a group of women met at Seneca Falls, N.Y., and began the U.S. woman suffrage movement with a catalog of "repeated injuries and usurpations on the part of man toward woman" called the *Declaration of Sentiments.* To prove men's having established "absolute tyranny" over women, and to bolster their claim that "women do feel themselves aggrieved, oppressed, and fraudulently deprived of their most sacred rights," the suffragists at that first convention itemized their grievances. They deliberately used the rhetorical model of the Declaration of Independence when they proclaimed, "We hold these truths to be self-evident: that all men and women are created equal." An excerpt illustrates the analysis of the feminists assembled in Seneca Falls and their sense of the ramifications of women's exclusion from full citizenship, specifically in ways that subordinated women. The suffragists complained that men's political practices regarded and rewarded women as inferior citizen-subjects.

> He has never permitted her to exercise her inalienable right to the elective franchise.
>
> He has compelled her to submit to laws, in the formation of which she had no voice.
>
> He has withheld from her rights which are given to the most ignorant and degraded men—both native and foreigners.
>
> Having deprived her of this first right of a citizen, the elective franchise, thereby leaving her without representation in the halls of legislation, he has oppressed her on all sides.
>
> He has made her, if married, in the eye of the law, civilly dead. . . .
>
> After depriving her of all rights as a married woman, if single, and the owner of property, he has taxed her to support a government which recognizes her only when her property can be made profitable to it. (Elizabeth Cady Stanton for the Seneca Falls Convention, reprinted in Kerber & DeHart-Mathews 1987, pp. 472–473)

The state, by excluding women from the franchise, jury duty, and other rights and obligations of citizenship, manufactured false differences between women and men as citizens. Exclusion reinforced men's privilege at women's expense—literally, in the sense of taxation without representation, and also figuratively. "But to have drunkards, idiots, horse-racing, rumselling rowdies, ignorant foreigners, and silly boys fully recognized, while we ourselves are thrust out from all the rights that belong to citizens, is too grossly insulting to the dignity of woman to be longer quietly submitted to," fumed Elizabeth Cady Stanton when she addressed the Convention (Stanton 1848, p. 32). Women's exclusion from full citizenship rights and benefits, from the equal protections guaranteed by the Fourteenth Amendment, and from participation in political life and exercise of political power governs gender by regarding, rewarding, producing, and positioning women and men vis-à-vis politics. Exclusionary measures view women as different from (gender polarization) and inferior to (androcentrism) men, frequently on natural grounds (biological essentialism). Stanton disparaged the difference as well as the inequality enforced by exclusion from the franchise. Throughout her career, she appealed to the common plight of men and women (not gender difference or feminine superiority) as justification for women's full participation in political life. She protested the ways states and social policies reinforced instead of redressed women's unequal status and power.

The intransigence of women's exclusion from first-class citizenship starkly limited Stanton's solidarity with other groups also excluded from political power. Phrases such as "ignorant foreigners" and "ignorant and degraded men" are red-flag terms in Stanton's justification of women's enfranchisement. One cost of women's political exclusion and the way the U.S. state governed gender was that some suffragists represented certain women as more worthy than many men. Stanton's attempts to emphasize differences of race, class, and nativity instead of gender exemplify the ugly consequences of the governance of gender for feminist politics.

As the twenty-first century began, women still could not vote in Kuwait, Saudi Arabia, Afghanistan, and other countries. States continued to govern gender by excluding women from the franchise, from executive political office, and from combat and therefore high command in the military. However, just as political scientist Nira Yuval-Davis reminded analysts of the military that formal inclusion "does not guarantee equality, either in terms of the actual tasks fulfilled by women or in terms of the power they exercise" (1987, p. 186; see also Goldstein 2001), exclusion does not exhaust the different ways states and social policies regard, reward, produce, and position women and men.

Constructing Gendered Citizen-Subjects

States and social policies govern gender through constructed criteria not only for the rights and duties of citizenship but also for benefit eligibility. Potential welfare beneficiaries have to decipher and conform to tightly circumscribed and often moralistic notions of gender, race-ethnicity, and labor. Dominant ideas about gender difference and male dominance determine eligibility for relief as well as political representation. Similarly, reformers—especially those who have historically determined eligibility and distinguished the worthy from the feckless—also confront gender (along with race-ethnicity, nativity, and class) as central features of their employment, their definitions of themselves, and their relations with clients, funders, and the public. States and social policies govern gender to the extent that among both reformers and their targets, both the rulers and the ruled, masculinity and femininity define key dimensions of credibility and power.

For example, historian Elizabeth Clapp (1998) showed that when Judge Ben Lindsey presided over one of the earliest juvenile courts in the United States (in Denver, for the first quarter of the twentieth century), he governed gender. He constructed boys as *delinquent* and girls as *deviant*. Delinquent boys maintained a sense of character to which the masculine judge could appeal. Deviant girls demonstrated the irreparable, and specifically sexualized, spoilage of their character, which the judge condemned. In addition, the women's club reformers who organized in Chicago even earlier than Judge Lindsey also contributed to the governing of gender through their work on the social problem of juvenile delinquency. As did many Progressive Era reformers, these women represented themselves as "mothers of all children" and used a powerful rhetoric of women's duty to care to justify the extension of women's activities beyond their own homes. Clapp traced the struggles between judges (all men) and probation officers (often women) over the construction of the juvenile court system. Those struggles typify the ways processes of state building, public service provision, and governmentality regarded, rewarded, positioned, and produced men and women differently as both clients and agents of the state.

Similarly, historian David Walkowitz (1999) documented the ways social workers deployed gender (and race and class) as they made expert distinctions between worthy and unworthy clients, and sought to establish themselves as professional providers serving paying and higher-status clientele. Throughout the twentieth century, social workers played a unique intermediary role as workers aspiring to middle-class incomes, working conditions, and lifestyles. They negotiated the space between poor people and philanthropic or government funding agencies. Social workers both presented social work as a professional activity and represented groups of clients in terms that reproduced gender polarization, androcentrism, and biological essentialism. Regina Kunzel's (1993) account of single mothers and social workers from 1900 to 1945 is another excellent historical example of this dual gendering through practice and policy, as is Barbara Brenzel's (1983) history of the first U.S. reform school for girls.

Historian of social work Karen Tice (1998) also showed how gendered social workers used gendered practices to construct gendered clients and thus governed gender through welfare practices eventually associated with the state. Starting with the early years of the twentieth century, Tice analyzed the case narratives that professionalizing social workers used to record their impressions of and work with "wayward girls" and "immoral women." Case recording constituted a gendered means of bringing gendered clients under increasingly bureaucratic scrutiny. Tice's research complements other historical work on the ways reformers and service providers—working to build both the welfare state and their own professional opportunities—governed gender through practices such as casework. Case recording as a method of describing, engaging, and ultimately constructing clients exemplifies the gendered governmentality I explained in chapter 2.

My own research on what feminist social philosopher Nancy Fraser (1989) calls expert "needs talk" (the language for translating daily life into professional practice and social policy) about single mothers and fugitive fathers bolstered historians' claims that agents of services central to the U.S. welfare state governed gender in their clients and in their own professional development. Social workers, public health nurses, and other case recorders used race- and class-specific gender criteria in their construction of "file persons," the basic unit of bureaucratic state management, created through case recording (think of both the Weberian and Foucauldian notions of bureaucratic and expert power I set out in chapter 2). In the process, case recorders from many disciplines discovered and gave meaning to the problem of single motherhood and the needs of poor women and children. They simultaneously marked individual women's conformity to notions of proper, capable, and deserving motherhood and carved a niche for themselves as reformers. Case recorders regarded, rewarded, positioned, and produced women and men as different and unequal—as clients, reformers, and employees of the U.S. welfare state.

Contributory and noncontributory state benefit plans (such as old age insurance, unemployment insurance, and workers' compensation) also govern gender. Such plans selectively benefit women and men who conform to gendered notions of work and family. Selectivity has important effects on the redistribution of wealth and the stratification of social groups along lines of class, race, and nativity as well as gender. Benefit plans govern gender through the ways they regard and reward women and men. For example, Madonna Harrington Meyer's (1996) analysis of Social Security benefits shows how spouse and widow benefits regard women as wives and mothers and men as workers. They reward men for their connections to the labor market and women for their connections to

wage-earning men. By regarding and rewarding men and women differently, such benefit plans reinforce both labor market inequalities and traditional (male breadwinner, female housekeeper) family structures.

Similarly, Alberto Arenas de Mesa and Veronica Montecinos (1999)
demonstrated the ways pension privatization (an important component
of economic 'restructuring' parallel to the proposal to privatize Social Security in the United States) in Chile aggravated gender inequalities. The
Chilean pension privatization process reinforced androcentric notions of
work and reproduced gender polarization in the divisions of paid and
unpaid labor in marriage. Through gendered double standards, state benefits and social policies regard men as breadwinners and women as wives
and mothers. They reward men and women differently, for conformity to
sharply gender polarized notions of worthiness and citizenship.

But policies and practices of entitlement and benefit eligibility do not
only *regard* and *reward* men and women differently. Programs also *produce*
gender difference and *position* women and men unequally. Ethnogra-
phers of the contemporary state in the United States have shown how.
Anthropologist Catherine Kingfisher (1996) observed welfare offices and
the groups of women (both clients and staff) who encounter each other
there. Her research documented how the criteria that determine welfare
eligibility and welfare recipients' efforts to represent their own interests,
factors that often work at cross purposes, both produce and position
women in gendered ways. Sociologist Lynne Haney (1996) compared the
ways two different state programs—one for juvenile offenders, the other
for poor young mothers—presented their clients with expectations about
normative femininity, motherhood, employment, and relationships with
men. She also showed how these two different groups of women resisted
the constructions of gender they felt were imposed on them. The variation
Haney found between her two sites contradicted the notion of the state
as a masculine monolith. Nevertheless, Haney's evidence substantiated
the claim that state programs govern gender through both policy and
everyday practice.

Perhaps most persuasively for the U.S. case, sociologist Renée Monson (1997) showed how the everyday practices for establishing paternity
and enforcing child support constructed women and men around gender-
polarized notions of work, motherhood, and sexual accountability. Child
support workers consistently collected much more intrusive information,
especially about sexual partners and practices, from women than from
men. In their case investigations—which often pursued details unneces-

sary to the bureaucratic paperwork that justified their inquiries—they questioned women more extensively than men, constructed women as both factually and sexually untrustworthy, "encouraged alleged fathers to state whether they were convinced of the mother's sexual fidelity," and focused on men as workers (1997, p. 292). In the same way that case records provide historical evidence of states' governing gender, the ethnographic observations by researchers such as Kingfisher, Haney, and Monson provide contemporary evidence of how the people Michael Lipsky (1980) called "street-level bureaucrats" construct proper femininity and masculinity.

A growing body of research also illustrates the contribution states and social policies make to the governance of gender with a specific focus on violence against women. Historians such as Linda Gordon (1986, 1988) and Elizabeth Pleck (1987) analyzed U.S. social policies about and practices to monitor and control violence against women and children as contested sites for constructing masculinity, femininity, power, and deservingness. Jalna Hanmer's interviews (with white, Pakistani, Bangladeshi, and Indian women in contemporary England) revealed the extent to which states and social policies designate, recognize, and privilege men as heads of households. They thus construct women as subordinate to men's authority, enable men to protect their own privileges, and protect violent men from criticism. Social service agencies and law enforcement contribute to the cultural "boundaries of acceptable violence" against women through interpretations of statutes, implementation of policy decisions, and rhetoric about 'family values' (1998, p. 138). Medical, counseling, welfare, and legal and police services provided by the state often "maintain dominant forms of agency policy and practice, or work within the dominant interests and definitions of men, or both," with the result of supporting rather than challenging men's violence against women they know (Hearn 1998, pp. 157–158). And as a growing body of anecdotal evidence, legal cases, and other research shows, welfare reforms, especially work requirements and time limits such as those imposed in the United States in the 1996 legislation, add to the points of leverage abusive men may use in controlling women's actions, earnings, and social networks and thus contribute to constructions of masculinity and femininity (see, e.g., studies collected by social work professor Ruth Brandwein 1999, the pioneering efforts of lawyer Jody Raphael 2000, and my own recent research 1999; 2000). In the ways states and social policies conceptualize, respond to, and regulate violence against women, they govern gender and its consequences for men and women.

Governing Gender from Womb to Tomb

It is not true that the only certainties in life are death and taxes. From your birth certificate and your elementary school registration to your driver's license, college financial aid application, passport, and marriage license, to your pension payment, long-term care insurance forms, and death certificate, you can be certain that the state is interested in your gender. Your classification as female or male, girl or boy, woman or man, on the paper trail and personal documents that officially record your life, is not merely for purposes of identification. True, gender (and race and age) are considered key identifying characteristics. The movies about women or men disguising themselves through cross-dressing, and the recent spate of histories and fictions about women "passing" as men, remind us that gender is considered a vital and generally foolproof identifying characteristic. But you can be certain the state is interested in your gender beyond simply trying to confirm that you are who you say you are. Gender is central to the ways states and social policies construct citizenship, democracy, welfare, nationality, and patriotism.

This chapter explored the many ways state institutions and practices produce, position, regard, and reward women and men as gendered political subjects. Juvenile detention and welfare programs aimed at young mothers construct notions of proper femininity. The everyday practices enforcing child support and determining welfare eligibility construct adult women and men around gender-polarized notions of work, motherhood, and sexual accountability. Moreover, state-sponsored institutions such as public schools socialize children into masculinity and femininity (as well as racial bigotry), as ethnographic observations of classrooms and playgrounds so vividly illustrate (Van Ausdale & Feagin 2001). Routine electoral politics produce quite different candidates and incumbents depending on their gender. For instance, men in politics seem only to have families when they are suddenly ready to retire from public life. The resignation rationale sounded especially clichéd in the case of Gaddi Vasquez, the Latino Republican county supervisor from Orange County whose career was seriously damaged by the fact that he oversaw the largest local government bankruptcy in U.S. history. Vasquez said he was forced from office not by the scandal but by his desire "to spend more time with my family."

Understanding how states and social policies produce and position women and men, gender difference and dominance, is an interesting end in itself for feminist state theory. Even more important, though, is the fact that understanding the governance of gender provides new strategic options for feminist organizing. If states govern gender through casework and through debates over economic development, through welfare policies as well as policies on violence against women, feminists have myriad points for contesting sexism (and racism, nativism, and heterosexism). Feminists may want to think twice (at least!) before invoking women's special capacities for care, nurture, peace, and moral purity as justifications for political power. My review of evidence of the ways states and social policies produce, position, regard, and reward women and men differently revealed the strongest sense in which states and social policies *govern gender*. But this is not all that applying a gender lens to governance shows. Not only do states govern gender. Governance itself is organized around gender difference, male dominance, and female subordination—my point in the next chapter.

CHAPTER 4

The Gender of Governance

Political sociologists have long debated the class character of the state and governance. In heated exchanges, pluralists and neomarxists, instrumentalists and structuralists, and others have argued over the extent to which states and social policies represent and enforce the interests of the dominant economic and social classes. They have wrestled to identify the conditions under which states and social policies are able to reconcile the short- and long-term interests of capital accumulation and political legitimacy, or to pursue relatively autonomous interests of rule and political organization. Americans are notoriously squeamish about class, and propositions about the class character of the U.S. state have often been dismissed as communist, or conspiracy theories, or both. To suggest that some or all of politics might be a form of 'class warfare' is, in the U.S. context, frequently considered divisive, unpatriotic, or paranoid.

Nevertheless, most U.S. adults acknowledge that in politics money talks, leadership is less about what you know than who you know, and "we the people" have relatively little say in national or global affairs. Even mainstream analysts see the rules of the game and organization of governance as benefiting incumbents and specific social groups or 'special interests,' including business. Analysts from positions as distant on the political spectrum as Comrade Vladimir Ilyich Lenin (1929) and free-market acolyte Professor Milton Friedman (1982) have cast parliamentary democracy as the political form most perfectly adapted to the perpetuation of industrial capitalism.

Political analysts have made three main types of arguments about the class character of the state: *instrumentalist*, *structuralist*, and *state-centered*.

Political sociologist G. William Domhoff (1998) persuasively put forth the view that those who govern are both drawn from and constitute a ruling class or power elite. Recall from chapter 2 that Karl Marx and Friedrich Engels (1970) compared the state to the executive committee of the capitalist class. Marx and Engels made a classic *instrumentalist* argument: The state is capitalist because it is a tool in the hands of capitalists. Neomarxists such as Ralph Miliband (1983), Nicos Poulantzas (1978), Göran Therborn (1978), and Erik Olin Wright (1978) have located the class character of modern states in bureaucratic mechanisms and technologies of management, and their role in and dependence on capitalism. This is a more *structuralist* argument: The state is capitalist because of how it is organized, not just who holds office. In contrast to structuralist and instrumentalist theorists, more *state-centered* theorists, such as Theda Skocpol (1979), grant noncapitalist class and other autonomous powers and interests to state actors and capacities. But irrespective of whether they think of the state as a tool, a set of institutional and organizational logics, or a contradictory ensemble of relatively autonomous social relations, not one of these critical theorists of the state imagines that states are neutral with respect to class.

The assertion of the nonneutrality of governance is more controversial when it comes to gender. Concepts from class analysis are often gender blind. As a consequence, they obscure the fact that power elites are overwhelmingly made up of men. The more obviously gendered language of reform activities seems trivial. Compare 'municipal housekeeping' with 'social engineering.' Which sounds as though it should be 'women's work'?! Even 'tinkering' with social policies sounds more serious, political, and masculine than 'municipal housekeeping.'

Besides, individual women have risen to prominence in settings as diverse as monarchies, parliaments, executive cabinets, state legislatures, and New England town meetings. If women have been queens, prime ministers, cabinet secretaries, state governors, legislators, mayors, and voting citizens, as well as guardians of public virtue and municipal housekeepers, perhaps governance is not monolithically masculine. At the same time, every U.S. president, and every major party candidate for U.S. president, has been a man, as well as a white Christian with a stereotypical nuclear family. This blunt fact of identity politics implies something about the racial character of the U.S. government, the shallowness of the separation of church and state, and the gender of governance. More than two hundred years of men in the Oval Office seems evidence enough to establish irrefutably the masculine character of executive political leadership in the United States.

At the same time, women leaders (and elected and appointed state officials) raise some very interesting questions about the gender of governance. How is *governance* gendered if one woman has made it to the top? How is *she* gendered—does she have to conform to masculine norms of leadership? Is women's token presence different from how governance is gendered if women are *half* the rulers, leaders, governors, legislators, party organizers, candidates, or voters for the winning candidate? Most important, is the gender of governance anything other than the proportion of women and men who are elected and appointed officials and employees of state bureaucracies?

In this chapter, I use examples from feminist research on states, politics, and social policies to address two sorts of questions. The first (analogous to the questions *instrumentalists* raise) asks if women are there, if women are half, and what difference it makes. Call this the *women in government* approach. The second (analogous to a more *structuralist* approach) asks how and when and to what degree gender polarization, androcentrism, and biological essentialism organize state institutions, political behavioral expectations, and policy practices. Call this the *gender of governance* approach. To address arguments and evidence related to women in government, I focus on 'representation' in politics. Representation is a key way to assess the notion that *the gender of governance consists of men's general monopolization of, and women's exclusion from, otherwise neutral state institutions and social policy practices*. I then turn to the notion that *governance is gendered whether women or men are the predominant incumbents 'where the power is'*. After a general discussion, I focus a gender lens on two structural features of governance: the "two-tier" character of many liberal welfare states, and the mythical and historical origins of the state.

Gender and Representation, or, How Many Women Does It Take to Govern in a Democracy?

One source of evidence of the gender of governance is the absence of women in government. Governing bodies (of nation-states or regional or global units, such as the European Union or the United Nations) vary in the degree to which they are open to influence by women's movement organizations outside the state or by women promoting policy from within. Feminist scholars and strategists debate the possibility of "state feminism," the political power of feminists in civil service bureaucracies (known in Australia as *femocrats*; see Eisenstein 1996), and the conditions that seem to make some states more responsive than others to feminist demands (see Mazur 2001; Stetson 2001; Weldon 2002). These are all, at some level, instances of the gender of governance as *representation*. As political scientists Mary Meyer and Elisabeth Prügl point out, the bottom line is that when women are excluded, they are unable to introduce "women-centered ways of framing issues" into governance. Nor can women "advance feminist agendas" if they cannot get over the threshold of political participation and representation (1999, p. 5).

Political scientist Hannah Pitkin (1967; see also Duerst-Lahti & Verstegen 1995) provided a typology of modes of representation. Before women's enfranchisement, for example, men directly represent women in legislatures, parliaments, and other deliberative bodies. This form of gendered governance assumes that men (as women's fathers, brothers, husbands, and sons) can be trusted to identify and act on behalf of women's interests (for a legal discussion, see Reva Siegel 2002, who calls this *virtual* representation). Through *substantive* representation, women's interests are subsumed into the interests of men. Substantive representation is therefore a prime example of androcentrism in governance. It is also the literal example of a (lack of) *women in government* argument. That is, women's exclusion, the corollary of men's substantive representation of women's interests, perfectly exemplifies the instrumentalist sense in which the state is masculine.

With women's enfranchisement, candidates and incumbents (still overwhelmingly men) become women's *formal* as well as substantive representatives. Women's electoral participation incorporates women's votes into the formal authorization and accountability of elected officials. Formal representation is the second type in Pitkin's catalog. The phrase "No taxation without representation" captures the gains women make with formal representation. The gender gap in voting (that is, women or men favoring one candidate over another to the extent that it comes close to the margin of victory) is a hotly debated contemporary aspect of the gender of governance as measured in terms of formal representation. After all, a candidate who owes electoral victory to the lopsided margin by which women voted for her or him instead of his or her opponent will presumably take particular care to represent women's interests formally in deliberation and legislation.

Interestingly, both Robert Jackson (1998) and Anna Harvey (1998) focused on formal representation as a key factor in political change for women. Recall my discussion of historical legacies from the previous chapter. Jackson claimed that party politics and other supposedly non-gendered dynamics gradually and inevitably erode political inequality between women and men, as exemplified by enfranchisement and substantive representation. Harvey argued that the conditions under which women gained suffrage in the United States established a legacy guaranteeing the insufficiency of substantive representation. Harvey is concerned with the way the conditions of winning substantive representation *perpetuated* certain aspects of women's political disadvantage. Jackson, in contrast, is eager to demonstrate the *decline* in women's political disadvantage. Their opposing conclusions notwithstanding, Harvey and Jackson share a *women in government* model based in substantive representation.

As women win an increasing share of elective offices in state and national legislatures, women of the dominant race-ethnicity and class frequently gain a measure of *descriptive* representation, Pitkin's third type. In heterogeneous societies, legislative bodies look more representative as they become more diverse. Descriptive representation is the numerical sense in which women remain poorly represented any place where they are fewer than half the incumbents, where they have less than proportional representation. Comparative politics scholar Walter Korpi (2000) noted that the dates of equal enfranchisement and figures on the representation gap in the legislature and government vary considerably between countries. However, nowhere have women achieved parity in descriptive representation. To the extent that states and social policies are meaningfully 'where the power is,' differential descriptive representation measures the relative political access and success of women and men, offering fairly clear proof of the importance of *women in government.*

Finally, women's absence or presence has *symbolic* value. People sometimes point to the election (or anointment or appointment) of a woman as signaling accomplishment, opportunity, parity, equality, or the end of androcentrism in governance. If analysts can point to *women in government*, it is a symbol of the decline of gender inequality. This is the last category in Pitkin's typology. If democracy is 'representative' government, how are women represented? Whether present in equal numbers or not, political representation is about the ways politicians and policies depict women and women's interests. Gendered symbols and practices bring women and women's concerns into government settings, state institutions, and social policies. This notion of representation goes beyond numerical counts or behavioral styles of women compared to men in government and leadership. As feminist political scientists argue,

> women have been largely absent from images of political leaders as well as from the set of practices involved with leadership and governance. [Representations of women in politics] inevitably ha[ve] to deal with the complexity of inventing a way for women to be understood both as women and as (potential) political leaders, something imbued with masculine gender. . . . [I]mage and symbols have much to do with attributes of leadership and governance. (Duerst-Lahti & Verstegen 1995, p. 214)

Gender is key to symbolic vocabularies and repertoires of images everywhere, including politics, a point historian Joan Wallach Scott (1999) made with resounding clarity.

Consider the symbolic value of being able to refer to President Clinton's appointed secretary of state, Madeleine Albright, as proof that even the State Department and foreign affairs are open to women's power and leadership and therefore gender neutral. To argue that Albright's appointment was a form of *symbolic representation* of *women in government* is not to claim that her gender or her symbolic value were the only reasons Clinton appointed and the U.S. Senate confirmed her. However, Albright clearly symbolized a point about the composition of his administration that President Clinton wanted to emphasize.

Or contemplate, as leftist feminist psychoanalytic commentator Jacqueline Rose (1988) encouraged us to do, the contradictory gendered symbol thrice-elected prime minister Margaret Thatcher presented to British voters. As head of state, the "Iron Lady" crushed the striking coal miners and their communities with heavy-handed police tactics. She advocated the return of capital punishment. She led a chastened, putatively postcolonial Britain to military victory in the Falkland Islands/Los Malvinas. All the while, Thatcher also railed against 'the nanny state.' She slashed welfare spending and 'privatized' social services, leaving care for the poor, the sick, the young, and the frail elderly to low-wage workers or unpaid family members, mostly women. The rights to kill, wage war, and police citizens are the ultimate gestures of state power and authority. States distinguish between legal and illegal violence—between murder and justice, among hooliganism, vigilantism, and policing, between honored veteran and war criminal—through the judicious rationality, control, and consistency typically associated with masculinity. Thatcher's

rhetoric and practices in favor of war, police brutality, and execution le-
gitimated her beefing up state violence and authority at the same time
that she was bashing 'big government.' Thatcher's example demonstrates
the importance of women in government to *symbolic* representation, and
shows the complex gendering of women leaders when the policies they
pursue are at least as militaristic, authoritarian, and rationalist as those
of their male predecessors.

The symbolic value of women's representation raises the fact that in
order to rebut gender blindness, analysts often use *women in government*
arguments. It seems straightforward to point out that government in general (everything from party leadership to candidates to elected and appointed officials to employees and military recruits) is literally manned.
Although it is not true of everywhere and all time that women have had
little presence in or influence on government, it has certainly been true in
the West since at least the city-states of classical antiquity. In revolutionary states, dramatic changes in personnel and political rule along with
ideologies of gender equality brought large numbers of women into politics. In eastern Europe under state socialism, women had much higher
descriptive representation than did their peers in Western democracies.
(Ironically, the eastern European transition to 'democracy' after 1989 reduced women's descriptive representation.) Even in populist and revolutionary states, however, few women have served in the highest ranks of
military and state bureaucracies. For example, in the Soviet Union, eastern Europe (as Sharon Wolchik 1989 demonstrates), Cuba and Nicaragua
(as both Maxine Molyneux 2001 and Margaret Randall 1974; 1978 show),
and Yemen (as Maxine Molyneux 1991 illustrates), class and gender inter-
acted with the characteristics of national political institutions to limit
women's political leadership.

Although women have everywhere and always birthed citizens and
leaders, and even been queens and elected and appointed rulers, women
have generally not equally shared—let alone monopolized—territory, force
of arms, or sovereignty. Absence is consequential. It is self-reinforcing,
a downward spiral (not, as Jackson 1998 maintained, inevitably declining).

Women are not present to add a range of female experiences to gender-
"neutral" policies, they are absent from posts to sponsor special-
concerns legislation effectively, and we seldom see them in leader positions and so continue to lack models who challenge our assumptions
about gender and leadership. All of this combines into greatly dimin-

ished influence potential and tenuous access to important avenues of social power. And these in turn combine through multiple and reinforcing mechanisms to make the current power arrangements more difficult. In circular fashion, the absence of women as political leaders contributes to the continued absence of women as political leaders. (Duerst-Lahti & Verstegen 1995, pp. 220–221)

It is a short step from noting women's absence overall to noticing, as R. W. Connell (1987) did, that the higher you look in the hierarchy that is the state, the more obviously male-dominated it is. This problem of (lack of) *women in government* is true in two senses, prestige and rank. First, the parts of the state most centrally associated with state power (the military, police, and treasury, for instance) are more male-dominated than other, less prestigious parts of the state (agriculture or human services). In the United States, women have been appointed secretary of agriculture and secretary of health and human services, but not secretary of defense. Second, the lower ranks of state organizations may employ or recruit women, especially in clerical or direct service positions. Consider elementary school teachers in public education, letter carriers in the U.S. Postal Service, clerical staff in magistrates' offices, or enlisted members and non-commissioned officers of the armed services. At these lower ranks, some occupations in state institutions are typically stereotyped as 'women's work.' At best, legal prohibitions on discrimination in hiring, pay, and promotion in government offices may encourage women's entry into relatively well-paid, secure, blue-collar occupations such as letter carrier or prison guard. In this respect, Robert Jackson (1998) is right that the organizational imperatives of modern bureaucracy often erode barriers to *women in government*. But the base of a state bureaucratic pyramid is often staffed by women, whose presence marks not the end of gender inequality but its historical and institutional reproduction.

At the same time, incumbents and candidates for leadership and administrative positions are much more likely to be men, even in settings where they supervise or are supported by women. Think of public school principals, supervisors and executives in state offices, judges and magistrates, or commissioned military officers. At higher ranks, prerequisites for government appointments and civil service jobs include graduating from the most prestigious universities, joining the right fraternal organizations, or having an intergenerational legacy of leadership and competent service. Until recently (and in some places and many respects, even now), men have effectively denied women opportunities to meet these qualifications, thereby rationalizing men's monopoly of state power.

When asked in the late 1930s what women could do to prevent war and the rise of fascism, feminist critic and novelist Virginia Woolf (1938) noted that Prime Minister Baldwin had recently praised women in the British Civil Service for their competence and discretion. However, the Civil Service *Almanack* of the day amply illustrated the absence of women from all but the lowest status (and—no coincidence—lowest-paid) civil service ranks. To Woolf, this was evidence, in part, of the exclusion of women from political power. If women were excluded from political power, she reasoned, women could hardly be held accountable for men's warmongering. Woolf also pointed out that the dearth of 'qualified women candidates' about which well-meaning administrators and human resources directors complain would persist so long as women had only limited access to the educational, social, and other advantages that qualified men for the 'pipeline' into government service (and rule). Woolf was invoking a classic *women in government* method for showing her male correspondent the gender of governance.

Indeed, as research in the United States by Meredith Newman has shown, nearly sixty years later, the pattern is similar. "Although women fill 46 percent of [U.S.] federal white-collar jobs, they hold only 15 percent of [upper level] positions. At the top of the federal government hierarchy, women hold only 12 percent of the Senior Executive Service positions" (1995, p. 142). Newman explained that women potentially interested in government service or state employment may face domestic constraints, lack of experience and education, and barriers from their socialization, prejudice, and negative perceptions. At the systemic level, segregation of opportunities, lack of mentors and networks, and harassment keep women in the place androcentrism designates: at the bottom of hierarchies (p. 143).

Public schools are not the Marine Corps. However, both are gendered state institutions. As I argued in the previous chapter, their gendered character derives in part from how they govern gender, producing appropriately masculine and feminine students, graduates, cadets, or officer candidates. But I argue here that the gendered character of states derives also from how men and women, masculinity and femininity, are represented and organized within them. The gender of governance—the default masculinity evidenced by the disproportionate overrepresentation of men in the state itself—appears glaringly obvious using this instrumentalist type of rebuttal to gender blindness.

Gendered Structures

Women's absence, numerical underrepresentation, limited power on marginal issues, and segregation as officials, employees, and agents of the state result from more than just men's conscious efforts to exclude women and to use the state and law to defend their power and privilege. Compelling as (lack of) *women in government* arguments may be, the evidence of the gender of governance is not just in men's monopoly and women's absence. A gender lens helps reveal the structural reasons for, and consequences of, women's underrepresentation. Women's limited presence in state institutions is a product of the androcentric organization of politics and governance. Sue Ellen Charlton points to the political "dilemma for women": Why should women clamor for inclusion in an institution that can never really be "ours"?

> [W]omen may benefit from specific state policies in both industrialized welfare states and also in undeveloped states, but they are objects or targets of those policies, with little or no say in their formulation and implementation. To change this situation in any fundamental way requires that women, like any disadvantaged group, have access to and influence over that state apparatus which is primarily responsible for devising strategies of economic and social development. But to gain access without transforming the apparatus—as all those who seek basic change acknowledge—is to be coopted, in this case by a political institution whose primary goal is its own maintenance and expansion. (1989, pp. 20–21)

The gender of governance includes questions not only about who will fill jobs in state and private agencies but also about the rules women have to follow, the size of their budgets, and who will listen to them and take them seriously. Political scientists Mary Meyer and Elisabeth Prügl (1999, p. 5) talk about the ways the rules of governance (codified and informal) "construct and reproduce notions of masculinity and femininity and associated power differentials," an important structuralist or *gender of governance* argument.

For example, there are so few women in elective office because some features of the structure of political opportunity—the rules of the electoral game—impede women's representation. Systematic limitations include few open seats, small numbers of qualified potential candidates, or refusal of party leaders to recruit women for winnable seats. Women are also deterred by increasing campaign costs and relatively poor fundraising performance and incumbent advantage. Perhaps the biggest impediment in the political opportunity structure in the United States is the single-member, "winner-take-all" election system. When elections are organized around party lists and proportional representation, where political parties can set and fulfill quotas for the number of women candidates, women have a better chance of getting into elected office. Unfortunately, proportional representation and party lists are not a panacea for gender inequality in politics. In eastern Europe, party officials often refuse to place women high enough on the lists to make it to parliament. However, women have become prime ministers in parliamentary systems in England, Iceland, India, Ireland, Israel, Norway, and Pakistan that gave them this sort of structural opportunity.

Similarly, governance is often divided along gender lines into 'foreign' or 'international relations' (war, peace, and trade, all considered important and masculine) and 'domestic' (health, education, and welfare, often considered comparatively trivial and feminine). Therefore, other structural barriers include the perceived costs of identifying with 'women's issues' or feminism, and a common focus at the level of national office on international affairs rather than the domestic issues more frequently associated with women candidates. Structural impediments shape recruitment, diminish the chances of winning, and constrain aspirations for women seeking public office. Even if these impediments do not disproportionately affect women and men as candidates, in the aggregate they keep the numbers of women elected officials low because they tend to perpetuate the (male-dominated) status quo.

Indeed, states are gendered in all the same ways that complex organizations are gendered, because states are complex organizations. For example, in all the ways that workplaces are gendered, states are gendered, because states are employers—in some places, the largest employer around. Gendered divisions of labor and occupational segregation characterize state bureaucracies. As I noted above, men tend to be at the top and women at the bottom of state hierarchies and chains of command. In addition, Meredith Newman found that women generally "work in either redistributive or regulatory agencies, agencies characterized as rule oriented. . . . Rule orientation may also indicate that women operate from weaker structural power bases, as people in general who have positions with weak bases are more likely to operate by the book" (1995, pp. 158–159).

What is more, as Sara Evans and Barbara Nelson (1989) showed in their study of government employees in Minnesota, women are concentrated in clerical and administrative support positions. In contrast, government engineering, construction, and maintenance jobs are filled almost exclusively by men. Even when state employees are unionized, such segregation creates a wage gap between women and men. There are two ways to remedy the wage gap caused by occupational segregation: recruit, hire, and promote men and women into 'nontraditional' jobs, or pay workers equally for performing work of equal value even if their tasks are not the same. The struggles over "comparable worth" in public employment and the sexual harassment of mid- and upper-level state managers and public administrators (see the multistate study by Rita Mae Kelly 1995) exemplify the ways in which gender structures state institutions and employment practices.

Feminist scholars of politics such as Desley Deacon (1989), Hester Eisenstein (1996), and S. L. Weldon (2002) also argue that women's political power is limited by the historically specific structural features of the states in which we finally attain elective or appointed office or a toehold in patronage and employment. Links to women's movement organizations and constituents outside the state, bureaucratic chains of command and institutional organization, access to centers of debate and authority, and command over budgets, personnel, and other resources all matter. They determine the extent to which feminists can overcome the legacies of exclusion and masculine privilege in politics (see also the empirical examples collected by Dorothy McBride Stetson 2001 or Amy Mazur 2001).

Another important gendered structural feature of some welfare states and social policies is what Barbara Nelson (1990) referred to as the "two channels" of social provision. The U.S. welfare state, for example, has a two-tier structure. The benefits and services associated with masculine citizenship activities—being a soldier or a worker—are relatively generous. They are administered with minimal intrusion, little stigma, and no means test (that is, recipients do not have to prove need or plead poverty in order to meet eligibility criteria). In sharp contrast, the benefits and services associated with feminine citizenship activities—being a mother or supportive wife—are stingy, intrusive, stigmatized, and targeted through means tests. In both cases, services and benefits are blatantly used to reward gender conformity and punish (with poverty, surveillance, and shame) women and men who stray from race- and class-specific notions of proper gender behavior and comportment. As Meredith Newman pointed out, "Women are more likely to need the services of redistributive agencies than are men. Men are more likely to be the direct recipients of public spending on highways (as owners and employees of construction companies), fish and game projects, and other distributive policy areas. . . . Gender power is also implicated in the understandings of what is perceived as a transfer of wealth and what is understood to generate conflict" (1995, pp. 148–149). It is also an important empirical question, the extent to which women's relative equality (in welfare states such as those in Scandinavia) is due to class-based party and corporatist arrangements or women's descriptive representation in government, to a commitment to women's liberation or to replacing the gendered tiers of welfare provision with a single, androcentric standard in which everyone is expected to work for wages. In the previous chapter, I pointed to the ways the double standards of social provision govern gender by producing, positioning, regarding, and rewarding women and men as different and unequal. Here, I am arguing that it is also important to analyze the two-tiered character of the welfare state as a structural feature of gendered governance.

Political and legal theorist Catharine MacKinnon summarized feminist structuralist or *gender in governance* (as opposed to *women in government*) arguments about the state when she asserted that "the state is male in the feminist sense" because it "sees and treats women the way men see and treat women" (1983, p. 644). The state, MacKinnon argued, has an epistemological standpoint. Legitimate legal argument, for example, requires distance, objectivity, detachment, and impartiality, all of which institutionalize masculine subjectivity as the standard of neutral universality. It is hard social labor to posit the particular (masculine) as universal and then erase ideological construction of an epistemological standpoint so that it appears natural, ahistorical, and inevitable.

MacKinnon's analyses of the laws on rape, woman battering, pornography, and prostitution placed violence against women and women's sexual subordination at the epicenter of structuralist feminist state theory. Through law, states regulate and manage—but do not forbid!—men's access to women's bodies for purposes of sex, reproduction, and entertainment. Thus, the standard used to determine harm to women—for example, the harm of sexual harassment at work—was (until feminist legal scholars fought for reform) quintessentially androcentric. Juries were instructed to assess whether pinup calendars, persistent requests for dates, threats of rape, or exchanges of job opportunities for sexual favors would harm or disturb the 'reasonable man.' Such legal standards and rules are central to what feminists perceive as the structural gendering of governance.

MacKinnon and other feminists have also long argued that the heart of the structural organization of states and social policies is the division between public and private. Recall from the discussions of liberalism in chapters 1 and 2 that the distinctions between public and private, between political and personal, in liberalism parallel the distinction between state and civil society. Marx claims that the distinction is *ideological*, defuses class antagonisms, and protects capitalists by obscuring the class interests of property and profit with rhetoric about 'private' enterprise. Foucault asserts that the distinction is *artifactual*, created as people built state institutions and forms of power and simultaneously created civil society in contrast. MacKinnon argues that the distinction is *material*; the state establishes a public realm where men's interests will set the standard, and leaves women unprotected behind a veil of privacy. The slogan *the personal is political* gives voice to the feminist claim that the ideological and material distinction between public and private, state and civil society, is a central dynamic of women's subordination.

Other feminist state theorists have located the gender of governance in the way states structure historical accommodations between capitalism and masculine domination. Some, such as socialist-feminist economist Heidi Hartmann (1981), argued that capitalist accumulation and patriarchal control of reproduction constitute "dual systems." Where the interests of capitalism and patriarchy coincide—for instance, in driving down women's wages relative to men—states leave well enough alone. Where the logics of capital accumulation and male domination are potentially contradictory—for example, in maintaining women's availability as both low-wage workers and unpaid mothers—states and social policies become the site of political struggles to reconcile or manage them.

In contrast, neo-Gramscians such as Anne Showstack Sassoon (1987) argue that political processes (states and social policies) piece together the frequently contradictory imperatives of capitalism and patriarchy. The result is not a system or seamless garment tailored to the specific needs of either capital accumulation or masculine domination. Rather, states and social policies in this model constitute a patchwork of temporary compromises. They incorporate some aspects of the common sense of everyday people into a system of "hegemony" that flexibly reproduces both capitalism and patriarchy as logics that organize social relations.

In these ways and many more, even when men are not the incumbents of positions of power in the state, the organization, assumptions, and practices of governance are gendered. In the remainder of this chapter, I discuss one last gendered structural feature of states and social policies: the mythical and historical origins of the state.

Gender Marks State Origins

Political theorists are famous for their origin stories. Classical liberals Thomas Hobbes (1909), Jean-Jacques Rousseau (1967), and John Locke (1952), for example, all had accounts of the 'state of nature' from which early man sought to escape (for Hobbes and Locke) or was lured through feminine wiles (for Rousseau). Recall from chapter 2 that these theorists sought to justify the liberal state as the guarantor of relatively orderly commercial and political relations among 'free and equal' individuals. At the same time, they sought to undermine the divine right of kings and the feudal absolutist monarchies that had consolidated rule in the North Atlantic countries and their colonies.

As feminist political philosopher Carole Pateman (1988) has brilliantly demonstrated, the elements of 'free and equal' personhood in classical liberalism are synonymous with masculinity (and with racial-ethnic privilege and property ownership). Liberal politics assume the difference between women and men and use that difference to define freedom itself. The difference between women and men gives meaning to the distinction between freedom and subjection (Joan Wallach Scott also made this important point 1996; 1999). The difference between women and men, subjection and freedom, also reinforces women's subordination through hierarchical gender differentiation. Catharine MacKinnon (1989) addressed this issue explicitly in her critique of liberal state theory, from a somewhat different perspective than Pateman.

As far back as their classical origin stories, then, liberal states have been structured around gender difference and dominance. They reinforced gender polarization by making gender difference the model and analog for incommensurable political differences (e.g., between subjection and freedom). Liberal states reinforced androcentrism by making men's access to women's bodies the central metaphor for contract, and as a consequence structured contract, consent, and rights in terms of gendered notions of domination and subordination. Pateman (1988) shows how this holds for both the labor contract and the marriage contract. Liberal states reinforced biological essentialism when they made rationality and self-possession central to contract and (all except Hobbes) assumed nature or the Creator endowed only men with those qualities. Political theorist Jacqueline Stevens (1999) noted this as well, and placed men's control over women's sexuality and fertility at the structural center of states and politics.

Similarly, although from a different perspective, the account by Friedrich Engels (1902) in *Origin of the Family, Private Property, and the State* links state origins and capitalist class relations to gender relations, specifically sexual access to women, the division of labor, and property inheritance. Gender difference, for Engels, became male dominance only when class societies subordinated women's reproductive capacity—and therefore women, fertility, and housework—to the productive capacities benignly associated with men and masculinity. According to the nineteenth-century anthropology on which Engels based his origin story, egalitarianism was the rule in the precapitalist societies that were Engels's equivalent of the 'state of nature' in liberal theories. Class hierarchies were rooted in a combination of property and the physical force required to defend, to consolidate, or to expand it. Men defended, consolidated, or expanded property and class privilege through force and patrimonial inheritance. Thus men built states through conflict and war and developed women's sexual subordination through monogamy and prostitution. For Engels, too, as both Catharine MacKinnon (1989) and Gerda Lerner (1986) note, the story of state origins is fused with gender difference and dominance.

Max Weber's (1978) related story of state origins combined two tales that philosopher Nancy Hartsock (1983) recognized as specifically masculine in their obsessions with virility and domination. As Wendy Brown aptly reconstructed it, one Weberian state origin story focused on the values and practices of "predatory sexuality, territoriality, violence, and brotherhood" that are characteristic of marauding bands of men who are the models for the warrior state (1995, p. 187). This aspect of Weber sounds remarkably like Hobbes's origin story, emphasizing government as a refuge from the state of nature, where life was violent and competitive, "solitary, poor, nasty, brutish, and short" (*Leviathan*, i. xiii. 9). Weber's other origin story highlighted men's authority in households, derived in this case from their ability to defend their families and property from those same masculine marauders. This other aspect of Weber sounds very much like Engels's account of state origins in masculine defense of the division of labor and private property.

In all these cases, men theorizing the origins of states seem largely oblivious to the social and political character of women's subordination that follows from their accounts. Many feminist political theorists have commented critically and at length on that oblivion, a form of androcentrism. The upshot is, in the theoretical accounts of state origins, gender appears central to the characters, plot, and outcome of the story, whether that centrality is taken for granted, naturalized, applauded, or condemned. But what about the origins of modern welfare states? What does their history suggest about the gender of governance?

Between 1889 and 1945, extensive networks of women in the industrialized countries of the North Atlantic, the Americas, Australia, and New Zealand toiled to construct the intellectual and institutional foundations of modern social welfare. These women sought to focus the attention of their respective national reform communities on the problems and needs of women and children. They labored to build professional credibility and opportunities. Sometimes their efforts reproduced the racism, class privilege, social control of immigrants and workers, and doctrine of separate spheres in gender relations that characterized the broader social order. Sometimes their efforts challenged or subverted one or more of these powerful dynamics, either in their personal lives or on a larger scale. Either way, these women's activities constituted vital contributions to projects of political and social reform, of professionalization (specifically in social work, health care, policy administration, and academic social science), and of building state institutions and capacities. Among the historians who have documented different dimensions of this process are Susan Pedersen (1993), whose book compared women's reform efforts between the two world wars in Britain and France, and the scholars of many western European and other welfare states collected by Seth Koven and Sonya Michel (1993).

In the United States, for example, reformers governed the recalcitrant urban poor, founded the welfare state, fought ethnic machine politics, sought to defend and expand their professional and expert terrain, framed social problems, and offered technical solutions or at least managerial containment strategies to the challenges of their day. In the process, they shaped and policed class boundaries, racial-ethnic relations, and gender anxieties. Moreover, reformers built their beliefs about gender (and class and race-ethnicity) into the institutions and practices of government itself. (Joanne Goodwin made this argument in her 1997 book about the origins of Mothers' Aid in Chicago.)

Elizabeth Clapp's history of the juvenile court and probation system marks the difference between male judges' deliberately masculine emphasis on "the importance of individual character developed through the example of a strong male role model" and women reformers' deliberately feminine emphasis on "the importance of nurture and protection in the child's own home supported by a probation officer, who was often female" (1998, p. 127). To counter what he perceived as the effeminacy of reform activity, Judge Ben Lindsey of the Denver juvenile court eschewed home investigation (specifically, home visits by probation officers, who were mostly women) in favor of enforced school attendance, job placement, and above all the salutary influence of the judge's own manly concern on the character and disorderly behavior of boys. Reformers thus built a gender division of labor—and hierarchy of state power—into the origins of one part of the state criminal justice system.

In the case of the public administration, Camilla Stivers traced gendered reform impulses, "one [feminine] in the direction of social justice and improving the lives of the unfortunate, and the other [masculine] toward rationalizing and regulating organizational, institutional, and societal processes" (2000, p. 5). Stivers's argument focused on the influence of gender on the dominant practitioners, self-definition, rhetoric, and tools of public administration—the gendering of governance. She noted the gendered division of labor in the administration of government and neighborhoods. Men worked in municipal bureaus of public administration and "cleaned up government corruption" using methods such as accounting, centralization, and oversight. Women worked in settlement houses and "cleaned up city streets and playgrounds" using methods of connection, experience, discretion, and involvement (pp. 16, 54).

In addition, Stivers documented and interpreted the gendered anxieties of reformers—particularly, their concern for maintaining a masculine image for reformers in the face of a central paradox. Reform, especially "cleaning up corruption," had a distinctly moralistic tone. Furthermore, both moralism and cleaning had distinctly feminine overtones in the Progressive Era. But femininity was anathema to municipal reformers who wanted to be taken seriously in the masculinized world of city politics. In fact, as Stivers pointed out when she used the history of public administration to critique its current practice, the femininity of reform remains stigmatized. Bill Clinton, Al Gore, and Joseph Lieberman all used the pseudoscientific (hence masculine) language of "reinventing" rather than "cleaning up" government. The legacy of gender in governance resounds from the origins of the welfare state to its present reform.

The Diversity and Specificity of the Gender of Governance

A gender lens reveals masculinity as the 'default gender' of governance. Ordinarily, the masculinity of governance is hidden behind the androcentric ideology of universalism. *Women in government* arguments do not take the position that the state is gendered if only a token woman is present; they take the position that men have gender, too, and their monopoly on leadership and power positions constitutes an important instance of the gender of governance. A gender lens also reveals assumptions about differences between men and women—gender polarization. *Gender of governance* evidence such as that assembled by Stivers and Clapp shows governmentality for the gendered process it is, rather than allowing unacknowledged masculinist assumptions about professionalism, bureaucracy, or power to render gender and male dominance invisible.

Both modernist critics such as philosopher Carole Pateman (1988) and poststructuralist critics such as historian Joan Wallach Scott (1999) point to the ways states and social policies rest on perceived differences between women and men as a marker of power. The ways states and social policies 'see' women, men, and gender difference constitutes one important set of evidence of the gender of governance.

As employer, as enforcer of contracts (including marriage as well as employment), as service and welfare provider, and perhaps above all as artifact of the division between public and private, states and social policies instantiate gender. The payoffs of masculine privilege include a wage gap that persists despite equal pay legislation. As enforcers of contracts, states construct gender difference, heterosexual complementarity, and the criteria for normative masculinity and femininity. The liberal rhetoric of the distinctions between state and civil society, public and private, is profoundly gendered. It ensures that men's violence against women both at home and in the workplace is largely protected behind a veil of privacy, providing both pecuniary and nonpecuniary rewards to men. Social policies have created and still maintain gendered double standards of welfare benefits, citizenship benefits and rights, and powers of incumbency. The different ways states and social policies regard, reward, produce, and position women and men contribute to the governance of gender.

The gendered coding of governance in the United States shifted somewhat after the attacks on the World Trade Center towers and the Pentagon on September 11, 2001. Politicians no longer rushed to dismantle the effeminate 'nanny state,' represented by coddling social workers, protective legislation, hovering bureaucrats, and interfering regulators. Instead, politicians fell over one another to praise the butch 'hero state,' represented by vigorously masculine firefighters, cops, and military reservists. New York City mayor Giuliani underwent a major gender makeover in the wake of 9-11. Before, incidents such as his crackdown on "squeegee guys" (men asking for spare change while wiping the car windshields of motorists stopped at traffic lights) and his support for racist police brutality cast Giuliani as a tough guy, one form of masculine leadership. His response to the attacks on the World Trade Center repositioned Giuliani as a compassionate father figure—another, quite different inflection of masculinity. He joined the 'heroic' state (ironically, by being rendered less aggressive and more protective)—but in a favored masculine instead of stigmatized feminine idiom.

The shift from effete to manly, or from anal rapist to avuncular protector, is still about gender. Both versions of the state, both versions of Giuliani, are gendered. Both reflect and contribute to valuing certain kinds of manliness at the expense of most women and femininity (either literal or figurative, as in the violently sexualized denigration of the poor, people of color, and other subordinates). The recodings of the federal government and Mayor Giuliani in the wake of September 11, 2001, different as they were, neatly illustrate the gender of governance. The shifts expose the historical specificity of gender, and its social construction, in the context of states and social policies. The gender of governance changes over time as a result of the actions of human beings engaged in both everyday activities and broader struggles over the meanings and practices of politics. The specificity of cultural representations of Mayor Giuliani (and President Bush, who also underwent a gendered transformation after 9-11) illustrates the variability and diversity—nonetheless structured around specific norms and power relations—characteristic of the system R. W. Connell (1995) called "hegemonic masculinity."

Gender includes masculinity. Women may act just like men, or feel they have to because they are held to androcentric standards of success.

None of the supposedly 'universal' dynamics that might explain states and social policies—for example, imperatives of competition over power, resources, money, and so on—is 'ungendered.' The default gender of governance is masculinity, and androcentric sleight-of-hand renders masculinity 'neutral.' Moreover, it is not only the presence or absence of women that genders governance. The organization of states and social policies around hegemonic masculinity builds gender into states and social policies as a structural feature—from the ground up.

To recognize both instrumentalist and structuralist characteristics of gender in governance, both *women in government* arguments and *gender of governance* arguments, as I have done in this chapter, offers feminist strategists many options. As *women in government* approaches suggest, electing and appointing women—specifically feminist women—into political office, especially at the pinnacles of state power, is one important way of changing the gender of governance. But focusing on the *gender of governance*, using a gender lens to analyze states and social policies, results in three points. One, to put women into 'where the power is' will often require changing the rules of the game. Indeed, it will often require rearranging divisions of labor, definitions of work and worthiness, and other structural features of government. Two, without considerable systemic change, women 'where the power is' will have every incentive to talk, act, and govern just like men. Simply putting women in positions of power has the potential for the kinds of perverse reinforcements of both gender and state power to which Jacqueline Rose pointed in the case of Margaret Thatcher. Three, to win not only power but justice and peace involves changing not just personnel (govern*ors*) but also practices (govern*ing*) and the institutions that set the limits and possibilities of rule (govern*ment*). This is because there is variability in gender. Not all women work for peace and justice, not all men seek 'power over,' but all are constrained by social practices and institutions. Feminists equipped with analyses of the governance of gender and the gender of governance may have hope of contributing to such transformations without inevitably reproducing the status quo.

PART 3

Toward Feminist Governance

CHAPTER 5

Changing the Subject

Feminists want representation to go with taxation. Feminists want the benefits and incentive systems created by welfare, regulation, and law enforcement to promote safety and solvency, wider opportunity, and more meaningful equality between women and men. Feminists want women to be able to participate in local, national, and global politics, want the female half of humanity to take part in democratic decision making, want women's rights to be considered human rights. Feminists want women to be able to think independently, to be sovereigns of our own actions, to speak our minds and be heard, and to participate fully in the common life. To achieve what feminists want, women presumably have to be effective political agents. This chapter uses the insights about the gender of governance and the governance of gender developed in the previous sections to assess the main way researchers on gender and welfare states have tried to position women as political subjects.

A woman's place is in the House . . . and in the Senate reads the classic bumper sticker. The pun upturns the assumption of women's domesticity, a recognizable place or *subject location* where women belong. Thus, the slogan plays with sexist expectations. But it is not just the relegation of women to hearth and home that seems old-fashioned (and therefore humorous in feminist reversal) in this slogan. The notion of 'woman's place' also assumes a singular *subject*, the *woman* of political representation, participation, and democracy.

There is apparently no coherent feminist political subject. This is no laughing matter. Pessimism about women's becoming any but the most contingent political subject has both empirical and theoretical sources.

The *empirical* diversity among women—differences of class, race-ethnicity, nationality, sexuality, disability, age, and the like, which shape life-outcomes, consciousness, and possibilities for change—undermines simplistic notions of sisterhood or unity among women. Challenges have emerged in the form of the voices of women considered invisible, subordinate, or disenfranchised in 'mainstream' feminist movements—for instance, working-class women, poor women, women of color, lesbians, and women in prostitution. Their critiques starkly illustrate the extent to which differences in social location, experience, and power undermine the possibilities of feminist solidarity and women's shared political subjectivity.

The discursive, postmodern turn in recent scholarship also questions the *theoretical* stability and unity of subjects and identities. In its more psychoanalytic versions, postmodernism posits an irremediably split subject. We are divided between conscious and unconscious mind, between self-conscious agent and object. In the feminist psychoanalytic accounts by Julia Kristeva (1986) or Hélène Cixous (1994), people achieve consciousness and sociability only by submitting to patriarchal disciplines. A split subject is incapable of attaining unified consciousness, let alone engaging in strategic political action (historian Joan Scott 1999 clearly sets out the version of this position articulated by French psychoanalyst Jacques Lacan 1977; 1992). The problem of the split subject resounds in a plaintive passage from poet and essayist Adrienne Rich. "Sometimes I feel I have seen too long from too many disconnected angles: white, Jewish, anti-Semite, racist, anti-racist, once-married, lesbian, middle-class, feminist, exmatriate Southerner, *split at the root*: that I will never bring them whole" (1982, p. 83, emphasis in original). Humans are complicated. It is hard enough to have a sense of wholeness in a self that is rife with contradictions, let alone figure out how to work in solidarity with others.

Fortunately, questioning empirically and theoretically the category of *woman* as the ready-made subject of feminism (or simply as a coherent referent) is not the same as denying that gender is a form of oppression. Questioning the epistemological or even the empirical coherence of the category of *woman* does not necessarily preclude feminist subjectivity or collective action to end gender subordination. In fact, political sociologists Julia Adams and Tasleem Padamsee (2001) suggest that feminists can enhance our understandings of gender and politics by analyzing the ways people use states and social policies to establish political subject locations, 'hail' or call to the incumbents of those subject locations, and designate appropriate affect.

According to Adams and Padamsee, states produce characteristic subject location sets, such as policy maker, citizen, voter, social worker, welfare recipient, cop, and immigrant. Those subject locations have affiliated with them specific feelings or motivations that people consider appropriate and desirable. The appropriate feelings for political subjects might include entrepreneurial spirit, with its scarcity mentality; patriotism, with sentiments of loyalty and sacrifice; or xenophobia and racism, which mobilize anxieties about national and ethnic privilege, boundaries, and purity.

The slogan *A woman's place is in the House . . . and in the Senate*, identifies the legislature as a gendered subject location in political life. The slogan asserts that women belong in elected deliberative and legislative institutions. Liberals might claim that women belong in politics *despite* women's stereotypical associations with home and family. Maternalists claim women belong in politics *because of* the insights and interests that derive from their being the designated caring, nurturing people in society. Either way, the slogan names a political subject location, and positions women as appropriate political subjects to fill it.

Examples of affect appropriate to gendered political subjects include manly courage in the face of military threat and feminine concerns with children's health and welfare. Incumbents of some subject locations are honored political actors—for instance military veterans, especially those decorated with medals of valor. Others are vilified—for example drug-addicted, unwed teen welfare recipients. Given the power of ideology, representation, and talk in politics, the number of actual incumbents in honored or disparaged subject locations may be miniscule but still dominate political discussion and the public imagination. In this chapter, I extend Adams and Padamsee's call for attention to political subjects into the concept of the *privileged subject* of states and social policies. I use the concept to explore the strengths and weaknesses of the way contemporary scholars (and to a certain extent activists and politicians) privilege the working mother as political subject.

Privileging the working mother is understandable. I spend the bulk of this chapter weighing the benefits and costs of constructing working mothers as the hegemonic subject of gendered political theory and research. I want to inspect states and social policies more closely through a gender lens by setting out the reasons the working mother has been such a popular subject in studies of gender and welfare states, along with some critiques. I conclude by noting three things. First, to view states and social policies through a gender lens means remembering that even without "adding women," states and social policies are always already gendered (usually masculine). In particular, the supposedly neuter subject locations of welfare states and social politics (e.g., citizen, worker, soldier) must be recognized as gendered. That way, when giving voice to women's experiences, feminists will not lose sight of male dominance or merely substitute one privileged subject for another. (Recall that this was one of the problems raised in my discussion of instrumentalist or *women in government* ways of thinking about the gender of governance in chapter 4.)

Second, I argue that many of the problems with privileging working mothers as the subject of feminist politics and policy analysis are political and theoretical. In particular, the strong socialist feminist tradition of much critical scholarship and policy practice overemphasizes work at the expense of other, *equally material*, bases of women's oppression—specifically, violence against women. There are a host of reasons why economic approaches to inequality seem advantageous for feminists. It can seem easier to represent women's subordination as socially constructed and politically remediable if it is rooted in contradictions between earning and caring, work and family. Many (albeit few feminist) models of men's violence portray it as natural and therefore unchangeable, or psychopathological and therefore treatable only at the individual level. Other models return the focus to economics by claiming that the best way to undermine male dominance—including battering and rape—would be to make women less economically dependent on men. But feminists impoverish our notions of gender, welfare, equality, and emancipation if we focus exclusively on work and neglect sexuality and violence as important aspects of male dominance and women's subordination.

Similarly, there were serious casualties of the sex wars—the intense debates over strategic feminist responses to rape, incest, battering, pornography, lesbian sadomasochism, prostitution, and workplace sexual harassment. As Rhonda Hammer trenchantly pointed out, in the 1990s the U.S. popular media fed a frenzy of "faux feminist" attacks on "victim feminism." A group of mostly young, mostly privileged women argued that feminist attention to violence against women and sexualized subordination was overblown, puritanical, alien to their experience, and not in their interests. However, as Hammer also pointed out, feminists cannot afford to back down in the face of backlash. Feminist analysts of gender and governance focus exclusively on economics at our peril. Privileging working mothers as the subjects of feminist state theory misdirects our approaches to states and social policies.

Finally, and perhaps most controversially, I argue that we can usefully change the subject of feminist politics from a specific, privileged subject (such as *working mother* or *battered wife*) to political processes. Movements for social change, organizations and institutions in and against the state, and the ongoing back-and-forth through which people develop their political consciousness and capacities all provide subject locations and affect sets for the appropriate subject of feminist politics: *women in struggle.* All these political processes and the subjects they produce can usefully be viewed through a gender lens. In short, I claim that the proper subject of feminist theory and practice is not the working mother or even women unmodified (to paraphrase Catharine MacKinnon 1987 and to follow bell hooks 2000) but women in feminist movement—a shifting, contested political process (Armstrong 2002).

Meet the Privileged Subject

The privileged political subject of gendered research on states and social policies is the working mother. Researchers privilege working mothers in part because the "concerns of gender" generally invoked by scholars of gender and welfare states are either very narrow (women's employment opportunities, day care, support for care workers, and motherhood) or very broad (citizenship rights). As a result, they ask questions such as those posed by political sociologists Julia O'Connor, Ann Orloff, and Sheila Shaver.

> Should states promote greater social equality? Should government modify or strengthen market forces? Should governments or private entities be the instruments of insurance against social risks? Should states respect 'family privacy' and the decision-making authority of corporations? Should governments recognize any sorts of group rights, or attempt to accommodate systematic differences among social groups? (1999, p. 1)

These are all good questions. Presumably, when feminists ask them, the answers are different from the answers typical of mainstream theory and research. After all, the answer to the question "Should states respect 'family privacy'?" may be quite different if asked by a feminist interested in stopping incest or wife battering than if asked by an American Civil Liberties Union lawyer bent on preserving men's rights to consume pornography via their home computers.

But the answers will not be so different, after all, if the definition of gender focuses only on biological essentialism instead of also emphasizing gender polarization and androcentrism (see psychologist Sandra Bem 1993 and my discussion in chapter 2). Focusing on gender as distinct from biological sex is vital because it conceptualizes women's subordination and male dominance as socially constructed, historically variable, and politically and economically enforced. However, it fails to give analysts much critical purchase in the task of theorizing the specificity of gender in the historical formation, everyday operation, and political reform of welfare states.

The thin notion of gender characteristic of feminist welfare-state studies provides little basis for organizing feminist projects to combat the complicated intersections of sexism, racism, class exploitation, compulsory heterosexuality, and other modes of oppression. In their eagerness to address the mainstream of political sociology, those who use such a definition limit the "concerns of gender" to contradictions between earning and caring. My approach looks at the governance of gender as well as the gender of governance. Scholars who use a thin notion of gender tend to focus on the ways social policies aggravate or ameliorate inequalities between women and men, rather than how political institutions and practices contribute to the construction of gender difference and dominance in the first place. Such researchers privilege the working mother as the political subject of feminist state theory.

Why does working motherhood dominate feminist research and activism on welfare states and social policies? Moreover, why is it a problem?

Different researchers place different emphasis on the two terms of *working mother* as political subject. Some focus on the issues of waged labor, emphasizing the *work* in working mother. In particular, some feminist critics focus on the androcentrism of the workplace. At work, mothers confront segregation, discrimination, sexual as well as gender and race harassment, and profound unfriendliness to nonwork commitments, including family life (see for example the research collected by Jerry Jacobs in the 1995 anthology *Gender Inequality at Work*). Recognizing workplace androcentrism is a legacy of the socialist feminist roots of much of gendered welfare regimes scholarship, and represents an important payoff to gendered analyses.

Other researchers focus more on the issues of unpaid familial and poorly paid commercial care, emphasizing a broadly conceived meaning of the *mother* in working mother. Commentators have found it especially fruitful to unpack the gender polarization, androcentrism, and biological essentialism embedded in notions of citizenship, as revealed by attending to care. As Theda Skocpol (1992) points out in the U.S. case, common-sense notions of citizenship contrast the contributions of soldiers and mothers to the nation, promoting gender polarization. Common-sense notions of citizenship neglect the value and labor of care, reproducing androcentrism (for examples of the gendered character of care, see the pieces collected by Carol Baines, Patricia Evans, and Sheila Neysmith in their 1991 book *Women's Caring* or Selma Sevenhuijsen's 1998 book *Citizenship and the Ethics of Care*). Common-sense notions of citizenship rely on naturalized explanations of women's duties, abilities, and preferences, reinforcing biological essentialism (see *Caring and Gender*, the Gender Lens book on care by Francesca Cancian and Stacey Oliker 2000, and the special issue of the journal *Gender & Society* on care in international perspective). These insights are the fruit of feminist attention to what Adrienne Rich (1986) memorably called "motherhood as experience and institution," and represent another important payoff to gendered analyses.

Of course, gendered caring responsibilities are not limited to mothers. Daughters and daughters-in-law, sisters and sisters-in-law, and other women are all recruited into care work, paid and unpaid. So are men when family circumstances mean they have to care for ailing relatives, or when temperament or political commitment draws them to occupations such as elementary school teaching and nursing (Christine Williams collected illuminating examples in her 1993 anthology). But by privileging working mothers as political subjects, feminist scholars have been able to drive home important points. Their research reveals gendered double standards of work and citizenship, and the ways states and social policies contribute to the gendered organization of social, economic, and political life.

Whether the emphasis is on *working* or *mother*, the hegemonic subject of gendered welfare regime studies is the working mother. I mean *hegemonic* in two senses. The working mother is the privileged subject of feminist scholarship, the subject about which researchers tend to talk and write. I mean *hegemonic* also in the sense that the experiences and contradictions of working motherhood organize how many researchers, activists, and politicians think about gender, labor, and states and social policies. In the rest of this chapter, I elaborate four reasons the working mother has become hegemonic in political sociology and welfare state and policy studies: precedent, demography, methodological convenience, and politics.

Success Follows Success

The first reason for privileging working mothers as a political subject has to do with precedent. The easiest way to incorporate gender into relatively new terrain such as states and social policies is to focus on the sites where scholars and activists have already successfully demonstrated gender happens: the family and the workplace. Working mothers bridge home and work, private and public. Working mothers thus transgress the presumptively 'separate spheres' of modern, industrial societies. Both on the job and at home, working mothers are a symbol of challenge and change, lionized by feminists, vilified by conservatives. Working mothers are the group whose double lives have motivated important research on gender as an organizing principle of production, reproduction, and the distinction between them. Research on working mothers has contributed to accounts of the gendered organization of workplaces, where employers routinely reward uninterrupted careers, require workers undistracted by domestic duties, and expect women to be decorative, emotional, and sexually available. The gendered organization of home and hearth is of course more intuitive, but working mothers also usefully challenge the myth of motherhood as wholly domestic and dependent.

Some feminists argue that *working mother* is redundant; recall the bumper sticker that proclaims *Every mother is a working mother*. Many non-feminists think working motherhood is a contradiction in terms; only un-feminine careerists, neglectful mothers, and women excluded from racialized privileges of heteronormative femininity work for wages. Either way, working mothers live the spillover of family life into work and politics. Working mothers are most constrained by what sociologist Arlie Hochschild (1997) termed the "time bind" that results from escalating expectations on the job and little relief from domestic responsibilities. Government efforts to regulate, ameliorate, mandate, or excoriate mothers' employment are obvious examples of blatantly gendered social policies. The issues facing working mothers therefore provide a toehold for policy analysts interested in extending the study of gender beyond the obvious realm of home and family, and the hard-fought territory of paid employment, to the terrain of the state.

Unfortunately, in the context of states and social policies, the focus on working mothers reinforces the bad habits of androcentric social science. Those habits reproduce the problems feminists continue to have with scholars such as Gøsta Esping-Andersen (1990; 1999). Esping-Andersen analyzes variation in what he calls "welfare regimes," that is, the combinations of markets, families, and states that are the preferred way for people to meet their material needs that vary over time and across countries (for an extended discussion, critique, and bibliography, see my 2002 essay in *Social Politics*; see also the 1999 book on liberal welfare regimes by Julia O'Connor, Ann Shola Orloff, and Sheila Shaver). Esping-Andersen relies on ostensibly universal notions of work and citizenship. Feminist research convincingly shows that both work and citizenship are in fact deeply gendered. Esping-Andersen and other mainstream political sociologists frequently assume workers and voters are men, with access to women willing to enhance their welfare with unpaid care.

It is as though by looking at the site traditionally associated with femininity—the family—nonfeminists such as Esping-Andersen are somehow analyzing women's lives or gender relations. It is as though masculinity—let alone male privilege or men's power—has nothing to do with it. It is as though it takes women's interloping on the otherwise neuter terrain of states and social policy by going to work (where all those male breadwinners really belong, but we didn't notice they were masculine until women started demanding equal opportunities and pay equity) to show the gendering of governance. It is as though the only way to value what women do is to analyze it in recognizably masculinist terms—for example, by reclassifying caring as work.

Political sociologists may *think* that if they are talking about work or social policy or liberalism or the market, they are being universalist. However, adding working mothers as the political subject of welfare state studies does not remedy androcentrism. Pairing the working mother with the putatively universal but obviously masculine citizen-soldier-worker—and thereby including both women and families in the realm of politics—is a step in the right direction in the feminist transformation of welfare state studies. But it is not enough.

Gender scholar Yvonne Hirdman made a similar point with reference to the Swedish case. Sweden, along with the other Scandinavian countries, is rightfully praised by many observers concerned with gender.

Swedes profess a general commitment to egalitarianism and feminists observe relatively high outcomes on measures of the status of women in Sweden. Women hold a high percentage of parliamentary seats in Sweden, women's labor force participation is high, and the gap between women's and men's wages is comparatively small (for a concise presentation that seeks to combine Esping-Andersen's mode of analysis and some of the measures of women's political, economic, and social status feminists have earmarked, see Korpi 2000).

Unlike Esping-Andersen and many scholars of gender and the welfare state, however, Hirdman did not focus on work-family arrangements as the most important dimension of gender in welfare state studies. Instead, Hirdman looked more at the revealing consistencies between women's experiences in economics and politics. For instance, during the period of what Hirdman called the "equal status contract" in Swedish policy (1976 to 1990), occupational segregation relegated women to part-time, low-paid, often public-sector employment. Similarly, during this period, segregation in Swedish politics relegated women to "the 'soft,' 'reparative' areas of policy" (1994, p. 33; see also Bourdieu 2001). Hirdman noted the similarity between gendered patterns of labor force participation and parliamentary representation. She argued the gender of governance in the Swedish welfare state is evident in the subordination of women across areas of social life. Her critique obtains even in a country like Sweden, with a social democratic welfare state ostensibly committed to political intervention in the private realm to redress inequalities. The gender of the welfare state, Hirdman asserted, is visible less in the contradictions of working motherhood than in the consistencies of women's subordinate status. I agree.

Demography and the Failures of Maternalism

The second set of reasons for privileging working mothers has to do with demography and everyday life. Most women are mothers. More and more mothers work, although few work full-time, year-round while their children are small (both mothers' employment rates and women as a percentage of the labor force vary across industrialized countries and around the world). Mothers, even those with access to a male wage through marriage or cohabitation, are increasingly experiencing one version or another of what sociologist Arlie Hochschild (1989) called the "second shift" that housework constitutes for employed women. Many struggle with a heavy burden of care, especially the generation of adults sandwiched between aging parents and minor children. And many face the dire consequences of the lack of respect and resources devoted to mothering.

Analysts committed to comprehending and improving the world from the social standpoints and subject locations of diverse women thus understandably gravitate to working mothers. Working motherhood is a widely shared, profoundly consequential, formative, potentially politicizing component of both women's everyday lives and contemporary social organization. Hence the appeal of working mothers as political subjects. Hence the revival of arguments and movements to support women's personhood and claims to integrity, dignity, security, and political voice on the basis of women's assigned responsibilities for care and assumed capacities to nurture, protect, and train. Hence the renaissance of maternalism—arguing for women's political participation on the basis of their experiences and concerns as mothers—as feminism in hard times (as very smart and funny historian Sonya Michel put it in a conversation we had at a conference in Sweden in 1994).

What's wrong with this picture? For one thing, women throughout the rich, industrialized countries are postponing both marriage and childbirth. Fertility rates among whites in the United States and in parts of western Europe and in most of the former Eastern Bloc nations (or their fragments) are below replacement. Motherhood, while as widespread an experience of institutionalized femininity as feminist scholars and activists are likely to find, nevertheless takes up ever fewer years in women's life cycles, at least in the countries that most political sociologists use as cases (Andrew Hacker 2000 provides a useful nontechnical review of these demographic trends).

In addition, the focus on working motherhood as an almost universal experience of gender raises problems when racism starkly shapes both employment and motherhood. On the one hand, for women of color living in racist societies, mothering can require heroic efforts to raise children equipped to deal with the hazards of surviving and thriving under conditions of white supremacy (Patricia Hill Collins 1994 explores this point extensively in the U.S. context). On the other hand, mothers of color often face deeply segregated labor markets and other forms of racialized institutional disadvantage that shape their opportunities and experiences as workers (Amott & Matthaei 1996). The intersections of these issues in the lives of poor women of color in the United States have been explored by historians such as Gwendolyn Mink (1994) and Joanne Goodwin (1997). As they demonstrate, the ramifications of racism for working mothers are especially important in terms of policies and practices in welfare states.

More disturbing still, political arguments that seek to empower women specifically as mothers tend eventually to substitute child welfare for women's emancipation as their last-resort grounds for making claims on public resources and respect. Such arguments are particularly vulnerable to co-optation by racist, nativist, eugenic, and religious forces with interests in women's fertility, sexuality, caring work, and labor power distinctly contrary to feminism. In the U.S. case, political scientist Gwendolyn Mink (1994) and historian Rickie Solinger (1992, 2001) make this point with particular eloquence. Historians Seth Koven and Sonya Michel (1993) collect critical examples from around the world.

Finally, efforts to mobilize women as mothers appear more successful in some contexts and substantive arenas than in others. Yes, maternalist activists have been behind important welfare and human rights movements (Ladd-Taylor 1994; Clapp 1998). Maternalists are particularly effective when shaming politicians for murdering or "disappearing" their children, as for example Marguerite Guzmán Bouvard (1994) or Jean Bethke Elshtain (1994) showed in the case of the mothers of the Plaza de Mayo in under the junta in Argentina, and Patricia Chuchryk (1989) noted in the emergence of the Association of the Relatives of the Detained and Disappeared (Agupacion de los Familiares de Detenidos-Desparecidos) in Chile after the coup in 1973.

However, the balance of evidence is that, in the context of severe constraints, maternalism leaves something to be desired as feminist politics. Maternalism has never appreciably increased the value of mother-work in the market or in the eyes of policy makers. Maternalists have had only limited success reaching across gulfs of class and race in defense of children (let alone of themselves or of women different from themselves). Maternalist arguments have never successfully gained the same privileges for women's sacrifices related to motherhood that men have obtained for their sacrifices as soldiers and workers. Maternalist attempts to win for women first-class benefits of citizenship, or to reorganize paid and unpaid labor, have been markedly unsuccessful. Feminism in general has had little more success, of course, which is why maternalism looks good when feminists encounter intense opposition. But the backlash against feminist mobilization, and the conservative tenor of our times,

ought not paint us into the corner of maternalism or of privileging working mothers as the subject of feminist politics.

Measurement Errors

The third set of reasons working mothers have been such a preoccupation
in gendered welfare state studies has to do with methods and measure-
ment in social science research. Cross-nationally comparable microdata
(individual or household) are generally limited to demography, household economy, and individual attitudes. Analysts distinguish between
women with and without children (the child penalty), married and unmarried mothers (the marriage benefit), men and women workers (the
penis premium), and those who espouse more versus less traditional
views of masculinity and femininity or enact more or less traditional divisions of household labor (the attitude lag) when, and mostly because,
they can. A protracted debate over aggregate measures of women's status
relative to men of their generation, class, race, and nation over time has
resulted in cross-nationally comparable macrodata. These measures focus
mostly on gender inequality in political representation and leadership
(the suffrage gap and the representation gap), education (the literacy gap
and the cap-and-gown gap), returns to human capital (the wage gap),
income security and welfare (the benefits gap and the poverty gap), and
labor force participation and occupational segregation (the glass ceiling).

As a matter of methodological convenience and egalitarian convic-
tion, macrosocial research on gender addresses women in *comparison* to
men. After all, men are also workers, parents, and citizens. They thus
provide the appropriate benchmark for assessing progress toward equality. The good news is that having cross-nationally comparable measures
of the variability in women's achievements and status relative to men of
their own age group, family, race, class, and nation makes it empirically
easier to rebut male chauvinism as natural, universal, and inevitable.

The bad news is that comparative research on gender seldom assesses
women in social *relation* to men. In particular, analyses of women's subordination (rather than mere underrepresentation in particular realms of
social life) are virtually impossible with the types of data at the center of
equality gap comparisons. The cultural, sexual, physical, and emotional
enforcement of male dominance goes unmeasured, unremarked, and un-
challenged. Even those analysts who discuss "body rights" as an arena

of gender relations tend to reduce women's subordination to biological differences from men, rather than power relations privileging men (see for example O'Connor, Orloff, & Shaver 1999). The focus on working mothers narrows consideration of "body rights" to reproduction, which for all practical purposes means a curiously unsexed motherhood. Hence the inclusion of abortion, pronatalism, and eugenics—all very important, and fortunately straightforward areas in which to link explicitly the concerns of gender to those of race, ethnicity, and nationalism. What is excluded is women's specifically sexualized subordination, for instance, pornography, prostitution, sexual harassment, rape, lesbian bashing, and woman battering.

Violence against women is important in the analysis of welfare, states, and social policies for at least three reasons. First, it is important because violence mars the lives of so many women. Yes, pensions, care work, motherhood, and labor force participation are all important. But based on the airtime these issues receive, you might reasonably conclude that heterosexual privilege, sexual harassment, rape, battering, pornography, incest, and prostitution either do not involve gender or do not affect welfare.

Second, violence against women obstructs "goals of democratic governments, such as economic development, welfare reform, public health, pay equity, and child welfare" (Weldon 2002). When violence against women is included in the notion of gender that scholars use to inspect welfare states, political scientist and feminist policy analyst S. L. Weldon shows that the "cross-national pattern of government response . . . is quite unlike the patterns scholars discern in relation to women and employment, or in terms of family policy." This should not be a big surprise to feminists, who after all have no problem with the notion that violence against women—and government response thereto—has important bearing on welfare states, democracy, and public life in general.

Third, taking seriously violence against women remedies a problem shared by androcentric welfare state analysts and many of their feminist critics. *The sources of welfare are not limited to states, markets, and families.* There are many examples of nonfamilial, nongovernmental, nonmarket welfare provision. Most of them involve solidarity and mutual support among people excluded from the benefits of or membership in states, markets, and families. To new immigrants, refugees, people living on their own, religious congregations, and racial-ethnic groups facing discrimination, all sorts of informal networks, volunteer organizations, and social movements have been sources of welfare. Feminist critics have long made this point in discussions of a variety of aspects in the history of welfare states. But the most salient example, because it illustrates the thinness of both the concept of gender and the notion of welfare in welfare state studies, is the largely volunteer, nongovernmental, nonfamilial feminist movements to shelter women battered by their husbands and boyfriends (my thinking here is particularly influenced by conversations with R. Amy Elman; see also Jalna Hanmer 1998 or Maud Eduards 1992; 1997). Simply put, if welfare includes women's safety, welfare—even for working mothers—is not limited to states, markets, and families. Indeed, where feminists cannot create options beyond those three sites, women's welfare, safety, and equality may be profoundly compromised.

Feminist movements to shelter women fleeing abusive husbands and boyfriends respond to the gap between the presumption and the reality of families, markets, and states as sources of women's welfare. True, the original refuges for battered women were in community centers and volunteers' households. However, they allowed women to escape battering without relying on their own family members for protection. They did not require official documentation, willingness to press charges, confrontations with police or 'family services' social workers, or conformity to impoverishing or humiliating government eligibility criteria. They improved women's welfare without relying on or appealing to state authorities. Prior to professionalization, they depended on volunteers and in-kind contributions, not paid staff trained in psychotherapy, case management, or nonprofit administration. Many original shelter staff members were themselves once battered. In addition to material and emotional support, the first refuges enhanced women's welfare with political analysis and opportunities for building self and community through activism. None of these aspects of women's welfare in the face of violence and abuse are accommodated in the supposedly exhaustive realms of states, markets, and families.

Some feminist comparative policy analysts use a more expansive definition of welfare. R. Amy Elman (1996; 2001) includes policies on sexual harassment, battering, and rape in her assessment of gender and welfare states in the United States and Sweden. Comparative policy analyst S. L. Weldon (2002) explains variation in policy responses to violence against women in thirty-six stable democracies as a function of the interactions between state institutions (women's policy offices within government, for example) and feminist social movement organizations. Other feminist analysts also make a critical point about the gender politics of the common notion of welfare.

> In most conceptions of welfare, the presence of a man in the family is presumed to benefit both women and children. The assumption of male beneficence is manifested in many different ways, from the condemnation of single-parent (meaning lone-mother) households as bad for children, to the prescription of normality in family life as being essentially *about* the presence of a man, and the observation that families without men are generally worse off materially than those with men. The *consequences* of patriarchy—women's inferior labor-market position, their economic vulnerability—are conflated with the *personal* help that may or may not be given to women and children by men. (Oakley & Rigby 1998, pp. 102–103; emphasis in original, citations omitted, spelling revised)

Women's welfare includes health, material resources, divisions of labor, social and emotional support, and respite from the stress of living with men. Therefore, assessments of women's welfare have to include relationships between men and women, the welfare benefits men receive from unpaid women, and the fact that single mothers bear the brunt of the economic, social, and psychological costs of sexist discrimination and condemnation.

Julia O'Connor, Ann Orloff, and Sheila Shaver, in their book *States, Markets, Families*, are careful to include "laws . . . which fail to protect [women] from systematic (but 'private') violence" among the several ways "state programs and social policies have a less friendly side for women" (1999, pp. 2–3). They note that, depending on which policies they inspect, analysts might "form a somewhat different picture" of welfare states and social policies—while the United States has an economic safety net full of holes, it has been an innovator in asserting women's body rights (pp. 4–5; they echo a point made in R. Amy Elman's 1996 comparison of Sweden and the United States). They acknowledge the effect of battering on women's poverty and economic dependence on men or welfare programs, and mention state support for rape crisis centers as evidence of gendered welfare provision in response to feminist mobilization. In this respect, they are certainly at the forward edge of gendered welfare state studies. Gøsta Esping-Andersen no doubt means them quite specifically when he acknowledges his "feminist critics" (1999). Their efforts go far to bridge the yawning gap between mainstream regime studies and feminist analyses of the state. But I suggest that like many other analysts (e.g., see the analyses collected by Dorothy McBride Stetson 2001 or Amy Mazur 2001), their downplaying violence against women by privileging working mothers ultimately helps domesticate feminist critiques of gender and governance.

The Politics of Women's Poverty and the Poverty of Women's Politics

The fourth reason for privileging working mothers as political subject is theoretical and political. Gender scholars seek to challenge mainstream scholarship and politics in pursuit of a prowoman, social justice agenda. Working mothers (especially when they are single) are a strategic choice for a privileged political subject because they are demonstrably among the most vulnerable to poverty and exploitation. Mothers need resources, including cash, with special urgency because they are largely responsible for child welfare. Motherhood renders women particularly exploitable workers. Working mothers are particularly vulnerable to involuntary part-time, low-paid labor because of their care duties. As political sociologist Myra Marx Ferree (1993) pointed out in the case of feminist politics in Germany after the fall of the Berlin wall, motherhood turns women into a problematic group of workers, with important consequences for labor policy as well as welfare more narrowly conceived. Privileging working mothers as political subjects draws attention to the gendered character of poverty, work, family, the crisis of care, and welfare policy.

The strategic choice of working mothers as a privileged subject is an important counter to the androcentrism of comparative welfare policy studies. Privileging working mothers reflects well on analysts' pragmatic efforts to address social justice for the people (women) most likely to be impoverished in welfare states that rely heavily on markets and families to produce welfare. Sociologist Karen Christopher's (2002) cross-national comparison of the poverty rates of single mothers and others drove home precisely this point. However, the strategic choice of working mothers as a political subject has some troubling implications. It glosses over the reality of violence against women and the extent to which women can be trapped by both poverty and abuse. At the level of both theory and politics, privileging working mothers allows politically concerned researchers to document and presumably fight women's vulnerability without actually talking about (let alone blaming) men, masculine privilege, or male dominance. This is important for coalition building, but it blunts the critical edge of feminist analyses—a tough trade-off.

Gender equality has replaced women's liberation—and specifically sexual equality—both as a demand and as an analytic category in much scholarship on gender, states, and social policies. The focus on working mothers that is so characteristic of the field obscures the harms of women's trading political power, citizenship benefits, and inclusion in the workplace for virtue and respectability. After all, much of the debate about working motherhood as a social problem is about 'good' mothers. 'Good' mothers means sexually respectable yet (hetero)sexually available mothers, a classic 'damned if we put out, damned if we don't' contradiction of heteronormative femininity. Of course, no one can deal with everything at once. Scholars and activists have to make choices. The choice to privilege working mothers is a strategic one that owes considerable debt to a long and important history of socialist feminism in the critical social sciences. However, the centrality of sexual subordination to women's fate (along with violence, economic vulnerability, occupational segregation and discrimination, and isolation behind the veil of familial privacy) means feminists cannot endlessly defer discussions of sexual subordination and violence against women. The loss is too great, even if it is incurred in order to appear respectable or reasonable in a period like the present during which pundits from left, right, and center alike posit waged work and marriage as the solutions to all personal and social problems.

Women in Movement

The political subject of mainstream political science, history, and sociology is masculine. However, mainstream analysts generally fail to recognize the gendered character of their research, theories, and politics. They also tend to think that as long as they do not claim to be talking about gender as a phenomenon, their work is neutral and unbiased. Feminists challenge the androcentrism of mainstream scholarship by bringing women and gender explicitly into the analysis. Of course, feminist approaches do not gender research or theory by focusing on women; mainstream theory and research, like political subjects, are already gendered. In large part, decentering masculinity in politics means changing the subject, that is, including women (and the site traditionally associated with women's power and subordination, the domestic) in the political. Specifically, gender scholars follow sociologist Dorothy Smith (see chapter 2) when they use a classic feminist epistemological tactic—viewing the world from the perspective of women instead of from some hypothetical objective distance that turns out always to be already gendered masculine—to gain an analytical point of purchase on welfare and politics.

As a genre, gender-and-politics studies not only maintain an almost single-minded focus on working mothers, but substitute child welfare and divisions of paid and unpaid labor for women's sexualized subordination. They operationalize gender in terms of marginal debates over who brings home the bacon and how to facilitate working mothers' combining their responsibilities for earning and caring. They downplay the construction of masculinity and femininity, and ignore the ways gender relations define and delimit power and privilege in the postindustrial workfare state. They omit sexuality, violence, and subordination almost entirely, and they do so at the level of method, theory, and empirical substance.

These problems result from the abandonment of the rich if contentious legacies of feminist theories in favor of the pallid but more palatable remnants of stratification theory, rational choice, and family sociology. The result is an analysis that can no longer plausibly be ignored by the mainstream of political sociology. Indeed, Gøsta Esping-Andersen and Walter Korpi have taken up exactly the gauntlet the proponents of gendered welfare state studies have thrown down. Their recent work perpetuates the illusion that by talking about family and household economy they are addressing gender. Unfortunately, the hegemonic approach offers too little to feminists interested in state power, social policies, and women's emancipation.

Privileging working mothers as the political subject of gendered welfare state studies condemns us to a logic of 'women as'—*women as* workers, *women as* mothers, *women as* caregivers. In the idiom of gendered welfare state studies, *women as* logic is limited by the confines of its socialist feminist origins. The problems with this legacy are legion. Socialist feminism assumes that the primary contradiction in women's lives is between caring and earning, not, for example, between male violence and compulsory heterosexuality. In a socialist feminist framework, states are gendered to the extent that they mediate between markets and families, not, for instance, to the extent that they create proper women and men and reinforce male dominance at work, on the streets, and in the House . . . and in the Senate. Socialist feminists' hopes for women's emancipation rests primarily on women's increased labor force participation, not, in contrast, on feminist organizing to end battering, prostitution, and rape.

As a variety of friendly critics pointed out when feminists debated these issues extensively in the 1980s, the socialist feminist framework has trouble accounting for the specificity of violence against women or women's sexual subordination. With working mothers as a privileged political subject, many studies of gender and the welfare state can barely see women as victims. The resulting focus on working mothers gives gender scholars the dubious credibility of being reasonable and not stridently obsessed with victimization. However, these benefits come at the expense of dealing straightforwardly with the notion that perhaps masculine privilege, male power, and men's violence are implicated in states and social policies. Not to see women's sexual subordination in the context of states and social policies means not to cast that subordination in political terms. That is a grave political and theoretical error.

Feminists have long argued that the coercive and corrosive powers of battering, rape, sexual harassment, pornography, prostitution, and the like come less from their sheer prevalence than from the ways they render women interchangeable and therefore threaten, humiliate, control, and domesticate *women as women*. Women's experiences of, vulnerability to, and capacities to resist violence differ enormously. Attending to that variation and its consequences shifts the ways scholars, activists, and service providers think about gender, welfare, and governance.

The absence of women's sexual subordination from gendered welfare state studies is tragically easy to explain. As Rhonda Hammer (2002) points out, the backlash against so-called victim feminism has included vicious antifeminist attacks on research and activism on battering, pornography, date rape, workplace sexual harassment, and more. True, antiracist feminists such as Beth Richie (1996), Joy James (1996), and Kimberlé Crenshaw (1994) have sharply criticized how the emphasis on the vulnerability of all women to violent victimization erased the diverse experiences of poor women, lesbians, and women of color, and thereby impoverished antiviolence policies. Women are not defined solely by violence and subordination. But to concede the point and retreat to privileging working mothers as the political subject of gendered welfare state studies ignores the realities of sexism.

Women are the original stateless people. As Virginia Woolf put it in *Three Guineas,* her classic feminist indictment of war, fascism, and patriarchy, "As a woman, I have no country. As a woman, I want no country. As a woman, my country is the world" (1938, p. 166). Reading Woolf reminds feminists that nationalism and statehood are not the only ways to assert collective peoplehood or to affirm individual personhood in the face of symbolic and literal violence and oppression. Woolf also pointed out that the responsibilities of women (specifically, the "daughters of educated men") to use our influence to stop war and preserve culture and intellectual freedom are fraught in states where women have been systematically excluded from public life and rule (that is, everywhere). Andrea Dworkin (2000) made a similarly sophisticated point about the gender of nationalism and imperialism in the context of building and defending the state of Israel. Feminists do not have to become nationalists or imperialists just to position women as a coherent political subject.

Am I suggesting the privileged political subject of gendered welfare state studies should be the *battered wife* instead of the *working mother*? Absolutely not. There is no singular masculine subject of mainstream political sociology. Whether model citizens, workers, soldiers, or slackers, men are allowed a multidimensionality that is the antithesis of the narrow options of femininity (virgin/mother/whore is the traditional iron triangle). Neither should there be a single privileged political subject of feminist scholarship or action. The political subjects of feminism are, to paraphrase Catharine MacKinnon (1987), women unmodified, in all our variation and difference.

Perhaps even more usefully, to follow Elisabeth Armstrong's (2002) suggestion, the political subjects of feminism are women whose experiences encourage feminist consciousness and collective action—women in motion, women in struggle, women who dissent. Armstrong sought to shift the emphasis in contemporary feminist theory and practice away from the problematic category of 'woman.' She reinterpreted theory, memoirs, and events of the U.S. women's movement (for example, the discussions of racism at a National Women's Studies Association conference). She offered two categories from classical marxist political theory and practice—"struggle" and "organization"—as ways of understanding diversity among women and the political and politicizing processes of mutually constitutive theory and action that make up the women's movement. The proper political subjects of feminism, in this view, are women struggling to understand and change themselves, their relationships, and the world.

Most importantly, this strategy involves shifting the emphasis from a particular category of women—a privileged political subject—to political processes. Gender is the political process through which masculinity and femininity are created and given meaning as social categories. At the level of individual experience, interpersonal and group interaction, and institutions (such as the state), gender shapes identity formation, collective mobilization, and capacities for struggle. These political processes, rather than working mothers or any other specific political subject, are what feminist politics and theories of governance can most usefully comprehend and transform. A political process approach is more in line with contemporary theories of gender (as power and organizing principle) than is *women as* logic. It thus offers feminists the opportunity to study gender and governance without recapitulating the problems associated with privileging the working mother as political subject.

To realize the transformative potential of viewing governance through a gender lens will require changing the subject and transforming conceptualizations of gender, welfare, and the state. Expanding the subject beyond working mothers would take analyses of the governance of gender beyond the confines of maternalism, household economy, and the gendered division of labor. Changing the subject would take seriously the masculine character of state institutions and social policies while simultaneously acknowledging women as bureaucrats, reformers, activists, professionals, and political actors. One important theoretical and empirical advantage of viewing states and social policies through a gender lens is that doing so undermines the notion of a singular, privileged political subject. At the same time, using a gender lens demands recognition of the androcentrism of political institutions, processes, and analyses. The subject is always already (albeit variably) gendered, usually masculine.

By privileging the working mother, past scholarship has begun to remedy the invisibility of *women* in politics. But to remedy the invisibility of *male dominance* requires using a gender lens to build on the lessons of research, theory, and activism that specifically think of gender in terms of power relations. A gender lens expands notions of welfare beyond states, markets, and families. A gender lens addresses the masculinity of the multiple subjects of politics as usual. In short, changing the subject would help transform conceptualizations of gender, welfare, and state by looking at governance through a gender lens—by investigating the governance of gender and the gendering of governance.

CHAPTER 6

Slouching toward Where the Power Is

Feminists expect a lot from policy research and state theory. After all, as I have shown throughout this book, social policies shape notions of masculinity and femininity, the experiences of women and men, and the balance of power between us. State theory offers means and methods for understanding and challenging business as usual. Comparative studies of states and social policies provide evidence for feminists' argument that women's subordination is not natural, constant, nor universal. In particular, feminist state theory promises to explain how politics and policies construct and position women as subordinate persons, citizens, workers, sexual partners, activists, and family members. Feminist histories of the state show women as active participants in politics and effective agents of social change. Most compellingly, state-oriented research and theory offer feminists the tantalizing prospect of strategizing for social change through direct engagement 'where the power is.'

Some feminists are skeptical about the usefulness of state theory, however. There are two sources of this skepticism: an activist critique of theory and a Foucauldian critique of power and the state. Some activists disparage the utility of theory for promoting feminist politics and organizing. After all, feminists mobilized on behalf of women long before academics engaged in abstract debates over the origins, structure, function, or gendered character of states and social policies. State theories appear useless to feminists in a political era in which state power seems either irrelevant compared to the power of multinational corporations and other institutions of global capitalism or inaccessible compared to the power of local and regional organizations. What use is a feminist theory of the state

119

when accessible power seems widely dispersed and there is apparently no coherent feminist political subject? Even the category of 'woman' is empirically and politically unstable. 'The state' seems too complex to theorize, too fragmented to study comprehensively, and too abstract to engage directly. As activist academic Judith Allen pessimistically concluded, "'The state' is too blunt an instrument to be much assistance (beyond generalizations) in explanations, analyses, or the design of workable [feminist] strategies" (1989, p. 22).

In contrast, social theorists who take their main cues from Foucault argue that taking states and social policies seriously merely reinforces traditional, masculine notions of power and politics. To cite a classic example, criminologist and sociologist of law Carol Smart (1989) relied heavily on Foucault when she argued that engaging in legal reform efforts merely increases the power of law. Legal knowledge is a key method of interpretation. Legal interpretation is a primary means of producing legitimate power/knowledge. Therefore, engaging with states and social policies—specifically through legal reform strategies—inevitably reinforces the power of law and lawyers, politicians and policy makers, rather than providing critics with an important point of purchase in political contests. For Smart, legal knowledge always and by definition disqualifies feminist knowledge. Similarly, political philosopher Wendy Brown based her feminist theory of the state in part on her political hunch that

> domination, dependence, discipline, and protection, the terms marking the itinerary of women's subordination in vastly different cultures and epochs, are also characteristic effects of state power and therefore cast state-centered feminist politics under extreme suspicion for possibly reiterating rather than reworking the condition and construction of women. (1995, p. 173)

If, as historian Joan Wallach Scott (1999) persuasively argues, gender is a form of power/knowledge, and if state actors are privileged 'knowers,' then it seems likely that feminist efforts to enact reforms through law and social policy will inevitably augment state power. Reform campaigns will always "reiterate rather than rework" women's subordination. This Foucauldian skepticism should give feminists pause before we try to smash the state. Our efforts may merely reconfirm the gendered power of states and social policies.

In rebuttal: State institutions, capacities, and ideologies have important effects on the everyday lives of women and men. The apparatus of rule shapes the prospects for equality, and constitutes an arena of struggle too important for feminists to dismiss or ignore. In a system of nation-states, the people whose human rights and dignity are most at risk are stateless people. Just ask Jews between the destruction of the Second Temple in 70 C.E. and the founding of the state of Israel in 1948, or Palestinians since 1948, or people in the former Yugoslavia. Just ask women when they are refugees or illegal immigrants. Ask women when they are not enfranchised to the extent of their male peers, for example in the United States prior to 1920 or Switzerland before 1970 or in contemporary Kuwait and Saudi Arabia. Or ask women when their countries are ruled not by a recognizable state but by local warlords or religious authorities, for instance in Somalia in the 1990s or in Afghanistan under the *mujahideen* and Taliban.

Even states that appear weak in the face of demands for structural adjustment by global financial institutions such as the World Bank and International Monetary Fund may build their capacities and institutions. For example, policing is an important state power that 'weak' states may develop. Externally imposed currency devaluation, export-led economic development, debt repayment, free trade, reduced expenditures on health, education, and welfare, and the like may spark protest and rebellion against local elites at least as much as against international organizations. Even as they slash expenditures for public health, politicians may increase police repression (and material and ideological support for military and paramilitary organizations) to maintain their grip on local power. The contradictory requirements of social control and democracy under conditions of externally dictated expenditure patterns and debt may lead to state-building of a completely different type than former colonial or imperial powers may find rhetorically acceptable. National elites may be able to comply with terms dictated by multinational corporations or the World Bank only if they build strong police states. That does not make those police, and the dictators they often keep in power, any less strong. Similarly, strongly 'free market' welfare-state slashers like Margaret Thatcher may bolster police powers to stop labor organizing and protests against privatization. Or "compassionate conservatives" such as George W. Bush may beef up 'national security' capacities simultaneously with their efforts to further dismantle the relatively paltry and punitive U.S. welfare state.

Both the effects of and responses to structural adjustment and privatization policies and resulting conflicts are deeply gendered and therefore of tremendous interest to feminist theorists and activists. Women often disproportionately shoulder the economic and social burden when politicians cut spending in health and education, subsidize export rather than subsistence agriculture, promote tourism or export processing zones, and crack down on squatters and street vendors. Moreover, as the materials collected by Sheila Rowbotham and Swatsi Miller (1994) demonstrate, women are often important activists in movements to resist and repair the devastation of structural adjustment.

Similarly, state-building projects in the midst or in the wake of war and massive social transformation can proceed in ways that more or less exclude participation of women and feminist definitions of, for instance, national security, welfare, and the common good. For example, Maxine Molyneux (2001) shows how in Nicaragua, after the victory of the Sandinistas, women had to work hard to preserve the memory of their participation in both the armed struggle and the local mobilizations that made the revolution possible. The memory justified their equal participation in postwar, revolutionary governance. The essays collected by Barbara Harford and Sarah Hopkins (1984) about the women's peace encampment at Greenham Common, England, show how feminist protests against militarism and imperialism can produce sophisticated analyses and creative activism challenging the war machine. More recently, women's organizations were excluded from the official negotiations in Bonn after the military defeat of the Taliban in Afghanistan. As a result, national security was defined in military and paramilitary terms rather than in terms of securing women's well-being, rights, and participation.

In addition, there is considerable evidence that governments throughout the industrialized democracies can respond to feminist demands, to different degrees, in substantive areas ranging from abortion to family policy to job training to violence against women. International women's organizations have used a series of conferences to develop what the United Nations International Research and Training Institute for the Advancement of Women (INSTRAW 2000) calls an "engendered political agenda" for "advancing the status of women" in terms of equality, development, and peace. All in all, citizens and scholars of politics cannot hope to understand and change governments and policies unless they consider how, when, why, and to what extent state institutions, regulations, and rhetoric reflect and constitute male dominance.

Governance through a Gender Lens

Because states and social policies are one site 'where the power is,' and because they shape everyday life and the conditions of struggle, it is especially important to look at them using a gender lens, that is, using a perspective attuned to the social organization of masculinity, femininity, and relations between women and men. Looking at states and social policies through a gender lens reveals the extent to which truths held to be "self-evident" rest uneasily on assumptions and practices that govern gender and gender governance.

Social policies, professionalization efforts, and other dimensions of rule are best understood as gendered phenomena. Such an institutionalist approach complements—in part because it helps explain through structural rather than biological or purely psychological means—studies of the gendered effects of states and social policies on women and men as individuals or members of specific groups. I have worked in this book to explain the effects of difference and dominance on everyday life through analysis of gender at the institutional level. People are increasingly familiar with the notion of "doing gender," with the emergence of gender and power in face-to-face interaction. Looking through a gender lens at states and social policies allows analysts and activists to understand "gendered doing"—gender as a principle of social organization (the gender of governance), and its consequences for citizenship, democracy, and everyday life (the governance of gender).

Looking at states and social policies through a gender lens also puts the political focus of feminism on the conditions of diverse women's flourishing. It moves feminist theory beyond Catharine MacKinnon's (1989) questions about the gendered character of the state (reviewed in chapters 1 and 2) and sets us to wondering: Under what conditions are diverse women most likely to flourish? A gender lens shows the ways states and social policies construct, limit, and expand diverse women's economic, political, and sexual possibilities.

Violence and the Achilles' Heel of Feminism

Because many mainstream theories of states and social policies focus on violence (in the form of war, militarism, colonialism, policing, and the like) without acknowledging violence against women, it is especially important to include analyses of gendered violence in feminist state theory. In this book, I have brought research on violence against women into the context of states and social policies in ways that focus on the consequences of the gender of governance for the everyday governance of gender. I have suggested that we move beyond *women as* workers, mothers, caregivers, and citizens to *feminists struggling* for equality, opportunity, safety, solvency, dignity, and integrity. Feminist strategies benefit from looking not just at women as working mothers, citizens, and welfare recipients, but also at women exploited and harmed specifically because they are women. Feminist strategies benefit even more from changing the subject from categories of women to the *political processes* of identity formation and collective action (see the previous chapter; see also Larson 1993a; 1993b).

Women lose when feminist theories and movements neglect violence and abuse. To neglect violence and abuse, to try to sweep them under the rug, is tempting for many reasons. The stories of victims and survivors are disturbing to hear. Violence and abuse are hard to measure and harder to explain, especially if (as most feminists and social scientists agree) the idea is to avoid exclusively biological or psychopathological models. Battering and rape render all women vulnerable, yet are varied and structured by race-ethnicity, class, sexuality, disability, and nation. Campaigns to end violence against women strike at the heart of male dominance in a different and perhaps more threatening way than policy debates over equal pay or child care. When antifeminists attack research on violence against women and dismiss organizing to stop rape and battering, they are (as Rhonda Hammer 2002 rightly argues in her analysis of "feminist impersonators" as backlash collaborators) doing the work of the patriarchy.

Issues of violence against women are not only the sparks that have ignited firestorms of criticism from antifeminists. Violence against women remains a fractious issue among activists and analysts who want to further the causes of feminism. Women calling themselves feminists disagree vehemently with other feminists' analyses of prostitution and pornography as violence against women, for example. They disagree over the appropriateness of tactics such as regulating prostitution in terms of 'migration chains' of 'sex workers' whose problems are analogous to those facing domestic workers. Self-identified feminist analysts find the empirical complexity of women's realities so daunting that they are unwilling to condemn sexualized exploitation and harm. The fashionable feminist obsession with 'resistance' exaggerates women's agency in unlikely places (such as strip clubs and free trade zones). Claiming solidarity with "bad girls," some feminists mount attacks on the moralism and social control they see in other feminists' campaigns against the traffic in women. These attacks are indistinguishable in their content and effects from those of the "pseudofeminists" Hammer rightfully condemns. As I noted at length in the previous chapter, much social science research on gender focuses on conflicts between earning and caring rather than battering, rape, and other abuse. In the context of backlash against feminism, maternalists argue that it is strategic to focus on harms to children and the elderly instead of harms to women as women. All these debates about violence against women are internal to feminism as well as grounds for attacks from antifeminists. They reinforce my fear that violence against women has become the Achilles' heel of feminism. Yet concerns with work, sexual subordination, care, and violence against women need not be perpetually at odds.

To Form a More Perfect Union and Provide for the General Welfare

The notion that states and social policies are irredeemably contaminated as sites for feminist theory and practice, or as remedies for harms to women, is widely shared. Whether the proposed strategy to address women's oppression is market privatization, legal recourse, social services, or political mobilization, many people think that states are part of the problem rather than part of the solution. The notion of what one group of political scientists and policy analysts calls "state feminism"—the responsiveness of policy makers, state institutions, and political outcomes to women's movement demands—seems like a contradiction in terms (see Stetson 2001). Thus, former political prisoner and activist academic Angela Davis asks how radicals—or just ordinary folks—can expect anything but repression from racist, imperialist, sexist, violent states. "Can a state that is thoroughly infused with racism, male dominance, class bias, and homophobia—and that constructs itself through violence—act to minimize violence in the lives of women?" Davis wonders (2001, p. 12). For both activist and theoretical critics, states are simply the wrong territory for feminists to engage in struggle. For some, for example antiracist social movement commentator Joy James, this point is especially stark in terms of violence against women, people of color, Jews, and gay, lesbian, bisexual, and transgendered persons. All are subject to physical, economic, and cultural violence by a U.S. state that denies them benefits, equality, and protection from hate.

Thin definitions of gender and welfare narrow the meaning of governance. Again, the general neglect of violence against women is one part of the problem. Are welfare states actually about producing or ensuring *women's* welfare? Or is women's welfare only a concern of androcentric welfare states insofar as states regulate diverse women's labor, health, fertility, maternal caring, and sexual accessibility? Violence against women further presents the dilemma of *policing*, another dimension of the gender specificity of welfare states revealed only when subordination (rather than equality) is central to the analysis.

Throughout the Americas, for instance, women have pointed to the ways police and paramilitary organizations take advantage of their authorized power to violate, exploit, and mock rather than protect and defend women. The life stories of battered women collected by sociologist Ann Goetting (1999) or medical educator Elaine Weiss (2000) show the extent to which men employed as police feel they can abuse women with impunity. In some countries, women have organized to demand women-staffed police stations as a rape-prevention strategy. Any state theorist who has spent five minutes defending clinics from antiabortion demonstrators or working with battered women in or out of shelters understands that the gender of governance includes the contradictions of women demanding that mostly male cops enforce court-ordered protections for women seeking (or providing) abortions or shelter from battering. In post-Taliban Afghanistan, it is men, not women, who are calling for the creation of a unified national military as the only way to foster 'national security.' For women, security may be jeopardized as much by state-sponsored masculinist militarization as by violence and exploitation in 'private.' As long as military and police practices and personnel are characterized by racial profiling, 'excessive' force, rape, domestic violence, and social conservatism, the problems of feminists relying on police and the state will persist. In this respect, I could not agree more with Angela Davis's skepticism.

But recent work on gender and welfare states suggests that state violence is not necessarily redundant any more than state feminism is necessarily an oxymoron. This is true in part because, as I pointed out in chapter 2, so much of what observers of states and social policies see depends on how they define power. For those who agree with Weber that force is always central to the definition of the state, it will be hard to disagree with Davis. For those who agree with Foucault that resistance is ubiquitous but also futile, it will be hard to see feminist victories in changed policies or institutional practices. Feminist hope for political change requires feminist notions of power and governance of the type I have presented throughout this book.

This is the paradox of liberalism: Women cannot be recognized as vulnerable lest we jeopardize our claims to equality. But women cannot be equal without some redress of the vulnerabilities that relegate us to second-class status. When feminists demand recognition of harms that are invisible or condoned in conventional politics, we find out how little our experiences count. Harm, like obscenity and beauty, seems to be in the eye of the beholder. But when feminists suggest a standpoint from which to view women's injuries, it sometimes turns out that, as lesbian working-class poet Judy Grahn (1978) says, there is "nobody there to testify." At least, there is nobody there whose experiences are recognizable by the blank stare of the state. That blank stare (known among feminist cultural theorists as the male gaze) is part of the evidence of the *gender of governance*—the myriad ways states and social policies are organized around principles that distinguish between masculinity and femininity, and privilege the former at the expense of the latter.

When feminists demand compensation for harms trivialized by their congruence with women's lot, we discover how small is the concern for our integrity, dignity, autonomy, and efficacy. Indeed, feminist legal scholar Jane Larson (1993a) movingly demonstrated that if women incur harm in the process of conforming to ideals or expectations of womanhood—if we are devastated when men exploit us or if we fall ill using products that prey on our desperation to discipline our bodies—our experiences are contemptuously dismissed. This is not a matter of "victim feminism." On the contrary, it is about recognizing that, especially without privileges of race and class, some women are indeed vulnerable because of their conformity to traditional notions of femininity. As Pauline Bart and Patricia O'Brien found, "learning to be 'feminine' . . . results in [women's] increased vulnerability to victimization" (1985, p. 58). Most importantly for my present purposes, viewing states and social policies through a gender lens—and then acting on what we perceive—is about being willing to use law, social policies, and other aspects of the state to make integrity, political efficacy, safety, and solvency accessible to all persons, including women.

When feminists demand change in the practices and institutions that harm women, we notice that the tools citizens ordinarily use for reform are often designed to perpetuate, not challenge, the status quo. This explains the feminist frustration with reformism, and contributes to the pessimism Angela Davis exemplifies. It is also the kernel of truth at the center of the libertarian, Foucauldian, and skeptical activist attacks on regulation, litigation, and other political mechanisms designed to improve women's chances of achieving equality. To make matters worse, when feminists demand protection, we are told to quit whining.

There is an odd double standard at work here, one that provides a final example of the gender of governance and the governance of gender. When it concerns what men traditionally do to participate in the polity—voting, or serving on juries or in the military, for example—the U.S. Constitution carefully separates the exercise of duty from select characteristics of the citizen, such as property ownership. (This is no longer the case with criminal status. Only two U.S. states allow incarcerated felons to vote, and permanent disenfranchisement of ex-felons is sufficiently serious that it could have changed the outcomes of recent senate and presidential elections. These effects are shaped by the race and class composition of the population of ex-felons, the vast majority of whom are men. See Uggen & Manza 2002.)

By contrast, when it concerns the activities that traditionally bind women to the social order—mothering, in particular—Americans do not hesitate to tie duty to race and property. States use social policies combined with poverty as levers to influence women's choices and behavior, for example denying federal funds for abortions for poor women by arguing that a woman's freedom of choice does not carry a constitutional entitlement to the financial resources necessary to make the choice real. No one dares any longer make voting subject to a work requirement (in the form of a poll tax, for example), let alone a literacy or sobriety test. Yet the gender dynamics of welfare reform in the 1990s in the United States subjected mothering to a simple property standard: Do not have children you cannot afford.

The gendered character of the link between citizenship entitlements and the consequences of individual decisions affects political expression and participation. Spendthrift men may vote, but poor women should not mother (or even have sexual intercourse, it is implied). Yet both voting and mothering are cast as gendered obligations of adulthood and full citizenship. Such double standards constitute examples of the *governance of gender*, or the way debates over and implementation of social policies construct gender difference and structure women's opportunities relative to male peers and relative to previous generations of women.

The question is: Are the devils of gendered regulation, welfare provision, and social policy worse than the deep blue sea of unregulated competition, where women's economic and sexual vulnerabilities have historically sunk the dreams of so many? The evidence this book presents of the governance of gender and the gender of governance suggests that states and social policies potentially provide leverage for tipping the balance of power in 'private' (commercial, familial, or sexual) relationships. States and social policies offer potentially accountable and democratic means of intervening in seemingly intractable strongholds of otherwise untrammeled male dominance and privilege. States and social policies are too important an arena of feminist mobilization to abandon simply because when we *use* state power, we may *build* state power. Feminists can ill afford to dismiss any such source of leverage. Maria Stewart, an early nineteenth-century Black American feminist, exhorted the disenfranchised: "Sue for your rights and privileges. Know the reason you cannot attain them. Weary them with your importunities. You can but die if you make the attempt; and we shall certainly die if you do not" (in Richardson 1987, p. 38). Maria Stewart's sense of urgency and strategy about engaging with governance still inspires.

Chapter One
Chomsky, N. 1994. *The prosperous few and the restless many*. Tucson: Odonian Press.
Gutmann, A., ed. 1988. *Democracy and the welfare state*. Princeton, N.J.: Princeton University Press.
Hindess, B. 1996. *Discourses of power: From Hobbes to Foucault*. Cambridge, Mass.: Blackwell Publishers.
Li, J. 2002. State fragmentation: Toward a theoretical understanding of the territorial power of the state. *Sociological Theory* 20: 139–156.
Piven, F. F., and R. A. Cloward. 1993. *Regulating the poor: The functions of public welfare*. Updated edition. New York: Vintage Books.

Chapter Two
Bachrach, P. 1980. *The theory of democratic elitism: A critique*. Lanham, Md.: University Press of America.
Barry, A., T. Osborne, and N. Rose, eds. 1996. *Foucault and political reason*. Chicago, Ill.: University of Chicago Press.
Beer, S. H. 1982. *Britain against itself: The political contradictions of collectivism*. New York: W. W. Norton.
Charlton, S. E. M., J. Everett, and K. Staudt. Women, the state, and development. In *Women, the state, and development*, edited by S. E. M. Charlton, J. Everett, and K. Staudt, 1–19. Albany: State University of New York Press.
Ezekiel, J. 2002. *Feminism in the heartland*. Columbus: Ohio State University Press.
Jessop, B. 1990. *State theory: Putting the capitalist state in its place*. University Park: Pennsylvania State University Press.
Lucal, B. 1999. What it means to be gendered me: Life on the boundaries of a dichotomous gender system. *Gender & Society* 13: 781–797.
Lukes, S., ed. 1986. *Power*. Oxford, U.K.: Basil Blackwell.
McCall, L. 2002. *Complex inequality: Gender, race, and class in the new economy*. New York: Routledge.
Offe, C. 1984. *Contradictions of the welfare state*. Cambridge, Mass.: MIT Press.
Wrong, D. 1979. *Power: Its forms, bases, and uses*. New York: Harper and Row.

Chapter Three
Abramovitz, M. 1988. *Regulating the lives of women: Social welfare policy from colonial times to the present*. Boston: South End Press.
Afshar, H., ed. 1987. *Women, state, and ideology: Studies from Africa and Asia*. Albany: State University of New York Press.
Brush, L. D. 1997. Worthy widows, welfare cheats: Proper womanhood in expert needs talk about single mothers in the United States, 1900–1988. *Gender & Society* 11: 720–746.
Ferree, M. M., W. A. Gamson, J. Gerhards, and D. Rucht. 2002. *Shaping abortion*

discourse: Democracy and the public sphere in Germany and the United States. Cambridge, U.K.: Cambridge University Press.

Haney, L. 1997. "But we are still mothers": Gender and the construction of need in post-socialist Hungary. *Social Politics* 4: 208–244.

Popay, J., J. Hearn, and J. Edwards, eds. 1998. *Men, gender divisions, and welfare.* New York: Routledge.

Sainsbury, D. 1996. *Gender, equality, and welfare states.* Cambridge, U.K.: Cambridge University Press.

Skowronek, S. 1982. *Building a new American state: The expansion of national administrative capacities, 1877–1920.* Cambridge, U.K.: Cambridge University Press.

Chapter Four

Brush, L. D. 1987. Understanding the welfare wars: Privatization in Britain under Thatcher. *Berkeley Journal of Sociology* 32: 261–279.

Kandiyoti, D., ed. 1991. *Women, Islam and the state.* Philadelphia: Temple University Press.

Kessler-Harris, A. 2001. *In pursuit of equity: Women, men, and the quest for economic citizenship in 20th-century America.* New York: Oxford University Press.

McCarthy, K. D., ed. 1990. *Lady bountiful revisited: Women, philanthropy, and power.* New Brunswick, N.J.: Rutgers University Press.

Steinberg, R. J. 1995. Gendered instructions: Cultural lag and gender bias in the Hay system of job evaluation. In *Gender inequality at work,* edited by J. A. Jacobs, 57–92. Thousand Oaks, Calif.: Sage Publications.

Wilson, E. 1977. *Women and the welfare state.* London: Tavistock Press.

Yuval-Davis, N., and P. Werbner, eds. 1999. *Women, citizenship, and difference.* London: Zed Books.

Chapter Five

Ashenden, S. 1997. Feminism, postmodernism, and the sociology of gender. In *Sociology after postmodernism,* edited by D. Owen, 40–64. Thousand Oaks, Calif.: Sage Publications.

Barrett, M. 1980. *Women's oppression today: Problems in Marxist feminist analysis.* London: Verso.

Fineman, M. A. 1995. *The neutered mother, the sexual family and other twentieth century tragedies.* New York: Routledge.

Game, A., and R. Pringle. 1984. *Gender at work.* London: Pluto Press.

Hamilton, R., and M. Barrett, eds. *The politics of diversity: Feminism, Marxism and nationalism.* London: Verso.

Harrington Meyer, M., ed. 2000. *Care work: Gender, class, and the welfare state.* New York: Routledge.

Litt, J., and M. Zimmerman, eds. 2003. Care in international perspective. *Gender & Society* 17.

McDermott, P. 1995. On cultural authority: Women's studies, feminist politics, and the popular press. *Signs* 20: 668–684.

Mitchell, J. 1974. *Psychoanalysis and feminism.* New York: Pantheon Books.

Rhode, D. L. 1995. Media images, feminist issues. *Signs* 20: 685–710.

Sargent, L., ed. 1981. *Women and revolution: A discussion of the unhappy marriage of Marxism and feminism.* Boston, Mass.: South End Press.

REFERENCES

Adams, J., and T. Padamsee. 2001. Signs and regimes: Rereading feminist research on welfare states. *Social Politics* 8: 1–23.

Allen, J. 1989. Does feminism need a theory of 'the state'? In *Playing the state: Australian feminist interventions*, edited by S. Watson, 21–35. London: Verso.

Althusser, L. 1971. *Lenin and philosophy*. New York: Monthly Review Press.

Amott, T., and J. Matthaei. 1996. *Race, gender, and work: A multi-cultural economic history of women in the United States*. Revised edition. Boston, Mass.: South End Press.

Arenas de Mesa, A., and Montecinos, V. 1999. The privatization of social security and women's welfare: Gender effects of the Chilean reform. *Latin American Research Review* 34: 7–37.

Arendt, H. 1951. *The origins of totalitarianism*. New York: Harcourt, Brace.

Armstrong, E. 2002. *The retreat from organization: U.S. feminism reconceptualized*. Albany: State University of New York Press.

Baines, C., P. Evans, and S. Neysmith, eds. 1991. *Women's caring: Feminist perspectives on social welfare*. Toronto: McClelland and Stewart.

Bart, P. B., and P. H. O'Brien. 1985. *Stopping rape: Successful survival strategies*. New York: Pergamon Press.

Beauvoir, S. de. 1961. *The second sex*. Translated and edited by H. M. Parshley. New York: Bantam Books.

Bem, S. L. 1993. *The lenses of gender*. New Haven, Conn.: Yale University Press.

Bensel, R. F. 1990. *Yankee Leviathan: The origins of state authority in America, 1859–1877*. New York: Cambridge University Press.

Blee, K., ed. 1998. *No middle ground: Women and radical protest*. New York: New York University Press.

Bock, G. 1983. Racism and sexism in Nazi Germany: Motherhood, compulsory sterilization, and the state. *Signs* 8: 400–421.

Borchorst, A. 1999. Feminist thinking about the welfare state. In *Revisioning Gender*, edited by M. M. Ferree, J. Lorber, and B. B. Hess, 99–127. Thousand Oaks, Calif.: Sage Publications.

Bordo, S. 1991. Docile bodies, rebellious bodies: Foucauldian perspectives on female psychopathology. In *Writing the Politics of Difference*, edited by H. Silverman, 203–215. Albany: State University of New York Press.

Bourdieu, P. 2001. *Masculine domination*. Translated by R. Nice. Stanford, Calif.: Stanford University Press.

Bouvard, M. G. 1994. *Revolutionizing motherhood: The mothers of the Plaza de Mayo*. Wilmington, Del.: SR Books.

Brandwein, R., ed. 1999. *Battered women, children, and welfare reform: The ties that bind*. Thousand Oaks, Calif.: Sage Publications.

Brenzel, B. M. 1983. *Daughters of the state: A social portrait of the first reform school for girls in North America, 1856–1905*. Cambridge, Mass.: MIT Press.

Brown, W. 1988. *Manhood and politics: A feminist reading in political theory.* Totowa, N.J.: Rowman & Littlefield.

———. 1995. *States of injury: Power and freedom in late modernity.* Princeton, N.J.: Princeton University Press.

Brush, L. D. 1999. Woman battering and welfare reform: The view from a welfare-to-work program. *Journal of Sociology and Social Welfare* 26: 49–60.

———. 2000. Battering, traumatic stress, and welfare-to-work transition. *Violence Against Women* 6: 1039–1065.

———. 2002. Changing the subject: Gender and welfare regimes. *Social Politics* 9: 161–186.

Butler, J. 1990. *Gender trouble: Feminism and the subversion of identity.* New York: Routledge.

———. 1993. *Bodies that matter: On the discursive limits of 'sex'.* New York: Routledge.

Cancian, F. M., and S. J. Oliker. 2000. *Caring and gender.* Thousand Oaks, Calif.: Pine Forge Press.

Charlton, S. E. M. 1989. Female welfare and political exclusion in western European states. In *Women, the state, and development,* edited by S. E. M. Charlton, J. Everett, and K. Staudt, 20–43. Albany: State University of New York Press.

Christopher, K. 2002. Welfare state regimes and mothers' poverty. *Social Politics* 9: 60–86.

Chuchryk, P. M. 1989. Subversive mothers: The women's opposition to the military regime in Chile. In *Women, the state, and development,* edited by S. E. M. Charlton, J. Everett, and K. Staudt, 130–151. Albany: State University of New York Press.

Cixous, H. 1994. *The Hélène Cixous reader.* Edited by S. Sellers, preface by H. Cixous, and foreword by J. Derrida. New York: Routledge.

Clapp, E. J. 1998. *Mothers of all children: Women reformers and the rise of juvenile courts in Progressive Era America.* University Park: Pennsylvania State University Press.

Collins, P. H. 1994. Shifting the center: Race, class, and feminist theorizing about motherhood. In *Representations of motherhood,* edited by D. Bassin, M. Honey, and M. M. Kaplan, 56–74. New Haven, Conn.: Yale University Press.

Comacchio, C. R. 1993. *Nations are built of babies: Saving Ontario's mothers and children, 1900–1940.* Montreal: McGill-Queen's University Press.

Connell, R. W. 1987. *Gender and power.* Stanford, Calif.: Stanford University Press.

———. 1995. *Masculinities.* Berkeley: University of California Press.

Crenshaw, K. W. 1994. Mapping the margins: Intersectionality, identity politics, and violence against women of color. In *The public nature of private violence: The discovery of domestic abuse,* edited by M. A. Fineman and R. Mykitiuk, 93–118. New York: Routledge.

Crittenden, A. 2001. *The price of motherhood: Why the most important job in the world is still the least valued.* New York: Metropolitan Books.

Davis, A. 2001. The color of violence against women. *Sojourner* (October): 12–13.

Deacon, D. 1989. *Managing gender: The state, the new middle class and women workers 1830–1930.* Oxford, U.K.: Oxford University Press.

Dellinger, K., and C. L. Williams. 1997. Makeup at work: Negotiating appearance rules in the workplace. *Gender & Society* 11: 151–177.

Domhoff, G. W. 1998. *Who rules America? Power and politics in the year 2000.* 3d edition. Mountain View, Calif.: Mayfield Publishing Company.

Duerst-Lahti, G., and R. M. Kelly. 1995. "On governance, leadership, and gender." In *Gender power, leadership, and governance,* edited by G. Duerst-Lahti and R. M. Kelly, 11–37. Ann Arbor: University of Michigan Press.

Duerst-Lahti, G., and D. Verstegen. 1995. Making something of absence: The "Year of the Woman" and women's representation. In *Gender power, leadership, and governance,* edited by G. Duerst-Lahti and R. M. Kelly, 213–238. Ann Arbor: University of Michigan Press.

Dworkin, A. 2000. *Scapegoat: The Jews, Israel, and women's liberation.* New York: Free Press.

Eduards, M. 1992. Against the rules of the game: On the importance of women's collective action. In *Rethinking change: Current Swedish feminist research,* edited by M. Eduards, I. Elgqvist-Saltzman, E. Lundgren, C. Sjöblad, E. Sundin, and U. Wikander, 83–104. Uppsala: Swedish Science Press.

———. 1997. The women's shelter movement. In *Towards a new democratic order? Women's organizing in Sweden in the 1990s,* edited by G. Gustafsson with M. Eduards and M. Ronnblom, 120–168. Stockholm: Publica.

Eisenhower, D. D. 1960. Military-industrial complex speech. *Public Papers of the Presidents, Dwight D. Eisenhower,* 1035–1040. Washington, D.C.: Office of the Federal Register, National Archives and Records Administration.

Eisenstein, H. 1996. *Inside agitators: Australian femocrats and the state.* Philadelphia: Temple University Press.

Eisenstein, Z. R. 1993. *The radical future of liberal feminism.* With a new preface and postscript by the author. Boston: Northeastern University Press.

Elman, R. A. 1996. *Sexual subordination and state intervention: Comparing Sweden and the United States.* Providence, R.I.: Berghahn Books.

———. 2001. Sexual subordination and resistance in comparative perspective. Paper presented to a special session on Women and Politics, American Political Science Association Annual Meeting, August.

Elshtain, J. B. 1995. *Public man, private woman: Women in social and political thought.* 2d edition. Princeton, N.J.: Princeton University Press.

———. 1994. The mothers of the disappeared: Passion and protest in maternal action. In *Representations of motherhood,* edited by D. Bassin, M. Honey, and M. M. Kaplan, 75–91. New Haven, Conn.: Yale University Press.

Engels, F. 1902. *The origin of the family, private property, and the state.* Translated by Ernest Untermann. Chicago, Ill.: C. H. Kerr and Company.

Enloe, C. 2000. *Maneuvers: The international politics of militarizing women's lives.* Berkeley: University of California Press.

Esping-Andersen, G. 1990. *The three worlds of welfare capitalism.* Cambridge, U.K.: Polity Press.

———. 1999. *Social foundations of postindustrial economies.* Oxford, U.K.: Oxford University Press.

Evans, P. B., D. Rueschemeyer, and T. Skocpol, eds. 1985. *Bringing the state back in.* New York: Cambridge University Press.

Evans, S. M., and B. J. Nelson. 1989. *Wage justice: Comparable worth and the paradox of technocratic reform.* Chicago: University of Chicago Press.

Ferree, M. M. 1993. The rise and fall of "mommy politics": Feminism and German unification. *Feminist Studies* 19: 89–115.

Ferree, M. M., and B. B. Hess, eds. 1987. *Analyzing gender: A handbook of social science research*. Newbury Park, Calif.: Sage Publications.

Ferree, M. M., J. Lorber, and B. B. Hess, eds. 1999. *Revisioning gender*. Thousand Oaks, Calif.: Sage Publications.

Fitzpatrick, E. 1990. *Endless crusade: Women social scientists and Progressive reform*. New York: Oxford University Press.

Foucault, M. 1977. *Discipline and punish: the birth of the prison*. Translated from the French by A. Sheridan. New York: Pantheon Books.

———. 1980. *The history of sexuality*. Volume I, *An introduction*. New York: Vintage Books.

———. 1988. The political technology of individuals. In *Technologies of the self: A seminar with Michel Foucault*, edited by L. H. Martin, H. Gutman, and P. H. Hutton, 147–162. Amherst: University of Massachusetts Press.

———. 1991. Governmentality. In *The Foucault effect*, edited by G. Burchell, C. Gordon, and P. Miller, 87–104. Hemel Hempstead, England: Harvester Wheatsheaf.

Fraser, N. 1989. *Unruly practices: Power, discourse and gender in contemporary social theory*. Minneapolis: University of Minnesota Press.

Friedman, M., with R. D. Friedman. 1982. *Capitalism and freedom*. Chicago: University of Chicago Press.

Frye, M. 1983. *The politics of reality: Essays in feminist theory*. Freedom, Calif.: Crossing Press.

Glenn, E. N. 1987. Gender and the family. In *Analyzing gender: A handbook of social science research*, edited by M. M. Ferree and B. B. Hess, 348–380. Newbury Park, Calif.: Sage Publications.

Goetting, A. 1999. *Getting out: Life stories of women who left abusive men*. New York: Columbia University Press.

Goldstein, J. S. 2001. *War and gender: How gender shapes the war system and vice versa*. New York: Cambridge University Press.

Goodwin, J. L. 1997. *Gender and the politics of welfare reform: Mothers' pensions in Chicago, 1911–1929*. Chicago: University of Chicago Press.

Gordon, L. 1986. Family violence, feminism, and social control. *Feminist Studies* 12: 453–478.

———. 1988. *Heroes of their own lives: The politics and history of family violence, Boston 1880–1960*. New York: Viking.

———. 1990. Introduction. In *Women, the state, and welfare*, edited by L. Gordon, 3–8. Madison: University of Wisconsin Press.

Grahn, J. 1978. *The work of a common woman*. New York: St. Martin's Press.

Hacker, A. 2000. The case against kids. *New York Review of Books* November 30: 12–18.

Hammer, R. 2002. *Antifeminism and family terrorism: A critical feminist perspective*. Lanham, Md.: Rowman & Littlefield.

Haney, L. 1996. The state and the reproduction of male dominance. *American Sociological Review* 61: 779–793.

Hanmer, J. 1998. Out of control: Men, violence and family life. In *Men, gender divisions, and welfare*, edited by J. Popay, J. Hearn, and J. Edwards, 128–146. New York: Routledge.

Harford, B., and S. Hopkins, eds. 1984. *Greenham Common: Women at the wire*. London: Women's Press.

Harrington Meyer, M. 1996. Workers or wives: The distribution of Social Security benefits. *American Sociological Review* 61: 449–465.

Hartmann, H. 1981. The unhappy marriage of Marxism and feminism: Toward a more progressive union. In *Women and revolution*, edited by L. Sargent, 1–41. Boston, Mass.: South End Press.

Hartsock, N. C. M. 1983. *Money, sex, and power: Toward a feminist historical materialism*. Boston: Northeastern University Press.

Harvey, A. L. 1998. *Votes without leverage: Women in American electoral politics, 1920–1970*. Cambridge, U.K.: Cambridge University Press.

Hattam, V. 1993. *Labor visions and state power: The origins of business unionism in the United States*. Princeton, N.J.: Princeton University Press.

Hearn, J. 1998. Men will be men: The ambiguity of men's support for men who have been violent to known women. In *Men, gender divisions, and welfare*, edited by J. Popay, J. Hearn, and J. Edwards, 146–180. New York: Routledge.

Hernes, H. 1987. *Welfare state and woman power*. Oslo: Norwegian University Press.

Hirdman, Y. 1994. *Women—From possibility to problem? Gender conflict in the welfare state—the Swedish model*. Research Report 3. Stockholm: Swedish Center for Working Life.

Hobbes, T. 1909. *Leviathan*. Oxford, U.K.: Clarendon Press.

Hochschild, A. R., with A. Machung. 1989. *The second shift*. New York: Avon Books.

Hochschild, A. R. 1997. *The time bind: When work becomes home and home becomes work*. New York: Henry Holt and Co.

hooks, b. 2000. *Feminist theory: From margin to center*. 2d ed. Cambridge, Mass.: South End Press.

Howard, J. A., B. Risman, M. Romero, and J. Sprague. 1998. Series editors' introduction. In *The gender of sexuality*, P. Schwartz and V. Rutter, ix–xii. Thousand Oaks, Calif.: Pine Forge Press.

INSTRAW. 2000. *Engendering the political agenda: The role of the state, women's organizations, and the international community*. Santo Domingo, Dominican Republic: United Nations INSTRAW.

Jackson, R. M. 1998. *Destined for equality: The inevitable rise of women's status*. Cambridge, Mass.: Harvard University Press.

Jacobs, J. A., ed. 1995. *Gender inequality at work*. Thousand Oaks, Calif.: Sage Publications.

James, J. 1996. *Resisting state violence: Radicalism, gender, and race in U.S. culture*. Minneapolis: University of Minnesota Press.

Johnson, A. G. 1997. *The gender knot: Unraveling our patriarchal legacy*. Philadelphia: Temple University Press.

Kelly, R. M. 1995. Offensive men, defensive women: Sexual harassment, leadership, and management. In *Gender power, leadership, and governance*, edited by G. Duerst-Lahti and R. M. Kelly, 195–209. Ann Arbor: University of Michigan Press.

Kerber, L., and J. DeHart-Mathews, eds. 1987. *Women's America: Refocusing the past.* 2d ed. New York: Oxford University Press.

Kingfisher, Catherine P. 1996. *Women in the American welfare trap.* Philadelphia: University of Pennsylvania Press.

Korpi, W. 2000. Faces of inequality: Gender, class, and patterns of inequalities in different types of welfare states. *Social Politics* 7: 127–191.

Koven, S., and S. Michel, eds. 1993. *Mothers of a new world: Maternalist politics and the origins of welfare states.* New York: Routledge.

Kristeva, J. 1986. *The Kristeva reader.* Edited by T. Moi. New York: Columbia University Press.

Kunzel, R. G. 1993. *Fallen women, problem girls: Unmarried mothers and the professionalization of social work, 1890–1945.* New Haven, Conn.: Yale University Press.

Lacan, J. 1992. *The ethics of psychoanalysis, 1959–1960.* Edited by J.-A. Miller and translated by D. Porter. New York: W. W. Norton.

———. 1977. *Écrits: A selection.* Translated by A. Sheridan. New York: W. W. Norton.

Ladd-Taylor, M. 1994. *Mother-work: Women, child welfare, and the state, 1890–1930.* Urbana: University of Illinois Press.

Larson, J. E. 1993a. "Imagine her satisfaction": The transformative task of feminist tort work. *Washburn Law Journal* 33: 56–75.

———. 1993b. "Women understand so little, they call my good nature 'deceit'": A feminist rethinking of seduction. *Columbia Law Review* 93: 374–472.

Lenin, V. I. 1929. *What is to be done? Burning questions of our movement.* New York: International Publishers.

Lerner, G. 1986. *The creation of patriarchy.* New York: Oxford University Press.

Lipsky, M. 1980. *Street-level bureaucracy: Dilemmas of the individual in public services.* New York: Russell Sage Foundation.

Locke, J. 1952. *The second treatise on government.* Indianapolis: Bobbs-Merrill Educational Publishing.

Lopata, H. Z. 1983. Women's family roles in life course perspective. In *Analyzing gender: A handbook of social science research,* edited by M. M. Ferree and B. B. Hess, 381–407. Newbury Park, Calif.: Sage Publications.

Machiavelli, N. 1977. *The Prince.* New York: W. W. Norton.

MacKinnon, C. 1983. Feminism, Marxism, method, and the state: Toward feminist jurisprudence. *Signs: Journal of women in culture and society* 8: 635–658.

———. 1987. *Feminism unmodified: Discourses on life and law.* Cambridge, Mass.: Harvard University Press.

———. 1989. *Toward a feminist theory of the state.* Cambridge, Mass.: Harvard University Press.

Martineau, H. 1988. *How to observe morals and manners.* Sesquicentennial edition with a new introduction, appendices, and index by M. R. Hill. New Brunswick, N.J.: Transaction Publishers.

Marx, K., and F. Engels. 1970. Manifesto of the Communist Party. In *Selected works in one volume,* 35–63. New York: International Publishers.

Mazur, A. G., ed. 2001. *State feminism, women's movements, and job training: Making democracies work in a global economy.* New York: Routledge.

Meyer, M. K., and E. Prügl, eds. 1999. *Gender politics in global governance.* Lanham, Md.: Rowman & Littlefield Publishers.

Miliband, R. 1983. *Class power and state power: Political essays.* London: Verso.

Mink, Gwendolyn. 1994. *Wages of motherhood: Inequality in the welfare state, 1917–1942.* Ithaca, N.Y.: Cornell University Press.

Molyneux, M. 1991. The law, the state and socialist policies with regard to women: The case of the People's Democratic Republic of Yemen 1967–1990. In *Women, Islam and the State,* edited by D. Kandiyoti, 237–271. Philadelphia, Pa.: Temple University Press.

———. 2001. *Women's movements in international perspective: Latin America and beyond.* New York: Palgrave.

Monson, R. 1997. State-ing sex and gender: Collecting information from mothers and fathers in paternity cases. *Gender & Society* 11: 279–295.

Muncy, R. 1991. *Creating a female dominion in American reform, 1890–1935.* New York: Oxford University Press.

Nelson, B. J. 1990. The origins of the two-channel welfare state: Workmen's compensation and Mothers' Aid. In *Women, the state, and welfare,* edited by L. Gordon, 123–151. Madison: University of Wisconsin Press.

Newman, M. A. 1995. The gendered nature of Lowi's typology: or, Who would guess you could find gender here? In *Gender power, leadership, and governance,* edited by G. Duerst-Lahti and R. M. Kelly, 141–164. Ann Arbor: University of Michigan Press.

Oakley, A., and A. S. Rigby. 1998. Are men good for the welfare of women and children? In *Men, gender divisions and welfare,* edited by J. Popay, J. Hearn, and J. Edwards, 101–127. New York: Routledge.

O'Connor, J. S., A. S. Orloff, and S. Shaver. 1999. *States, markets, families: Gender, liberalism and social policy in Australia, Canada, Great Britain and the United States.* Cambridge, U.K.: Cambridge University Press.

Orwell, G. 1949. *Nineteen eighty-four, a novel.* First American edition. New York: Harcourt, Brace.

Parsons, T. 1955. The American family: Its relation to personality and to the social structure. In *Family, socialization, and interaction process,* edited by T. Parsons and R. F. Bales, 3–34. New York: Free Press.

Pateman, C. 1988. *The sexual contract.* Stanford, Calif.: Stanford University Press.

Pedersen, S. 1993. *Family, dependence, and the origins of the welfare state: Britain and France, 1914–1945.* Cambridge, U.K.: Cambridge University Press.

Pitkin, H. F. 1967. *Concepts of representation.* Berkeley: University of California Press.

Pleck, E. H. 1987. *Domestic tyranny: The making of social policy against family violence from colonial times to the present.* New York: Oxford University Press.

Poulantzas, N. 1978. *Political power and social classes.* Translated by T. O'Hagan with the assistance of D. McLellan, A. de Casparis, and B. Grogan. London: Verso.

Randall, M. 1974. *Cuban women now: Interviews with Cuban women.* Toronto: Women's Press.

———. 1978. *Doris Tijerino: Inside the Nicaraguan revolution.* Translated by Elinor Randall. Vancouver, B.C.: New Star Books.

Raphael, J. 2000. *Saving Bernice: Battered women, welfare, and poverty.* Boston, Mass.: Northeastern University Press.

Restuccia, F. L. 2000. *Melancholics in love: Representing women's depression and domestic abuse.* Lanham, Md.: Rowman & Littlefield Publishers.

Rich, A. 1986. *Of woman born: Motherhood as experience and institution.* Tenth anniversary edition. New York: W. W. Norton.

———. 1982. Split at the root. In *Nice Jewish girls: A lesbian anthology,* edited by E. T. Beck, 67–84. Trumansburg, N.Y.: The Crossing Press.

Richardson, M., ed. 1987. *Maria W. Stewart, America's first Black woman political writer.* Bloomington: Indiana University Press.

Richie, B. 1996. *Compelled to crime: The gender entrapment of battered Black women.* New York: Routledge.

Ridgeway, C. L. 1997. Interaction and the conservation of gender inequality: Considering employment. *American Sociological Review* 62: 218–235.

Rose, J. 1988. Margaret Thatcher and Ruth Ellis. *New Formations* 6: 3–29.

Rothman, B. K. 1989. *Recreating motherhood: ideology and technology in a patriarchal society.* New York: W. W. Norton.

Rousseau, J.-J. 1967. *The social contract.* New York: Washington Square Press.

Rowbotham, S., and S. Miller, eds. 1994. *Dignity and daily bread: New forms of economic organising among poor women in the Third World and the First.* New York: Routledge.

Rubin, G. 1975. The traffic in women. In *Toward an anthropology of women,* edited by R. R. Reiter, 157–210. New York: Monthly Review Press.

Sassoon, A. S., ed. 1987. *Women and the state: The shifting boundaries of public and private.* London: Hutchinson Education.

Scott, J. W. 1988. *Gender and the politics of history.* New York: Columbia University Press.

———. 1996. *Only paradoxes to offer: French feminists and the rights of man.* Cambridge, Mass.: Harvard University Press.

———. 1999. Some reflections on gender and politics. In *Revisioning gender,* edited by M. M. Ferree, J. Lorber, and B. B. Hess, 70–96. Thousand Oaks, Calif.: Sage Publications.

Sevenhuijsen, S. 1998. *Citizenship and the ethics of care: Feminist considerations on justice, morality and politics.* New York: Routledge.

Shefter, M. 1977. Party and patronage: Germany, England, and Italy. *Politics and Society* 7: 403–451.

———. 1978. Party, bureaucracy, and political change in the United States. In *Political parties: Development and decay,* edited by L. Maisel and J. Cooper, 211–265. Beverly Hills, Calif.: Sage Publications.

Siegel, R. 2002. She the people: The Nineteenth Amendment, sex equality, federalism, and the family. *Harvard Law Review* 115: 947–1046.

Sklar, K. K. 1993. The historical foundations of women's power in the creation of the American welfare state, 1830–1930. In *Mothers of a new world: Maternalist politics and the origins of welfare states,* edited by S. Koven and S. Michel, 43–93. New York: Routledge.

———. 1995. *Florence Kelley and the nation's work.* New Haven, Conn.: Yale University Press.

Skocpol, T. 1979. *States and social revolutions: A comparative analysis of France, Russia, and China.* New York: Cambridge University Press.

———. 1992. *Protecting soldiers and mothers: The political origins of social policy in the United States*. Cambridge, Mass.: Belknap Press of Harvard University Press.

Smart, C. 1989. *Feminism and the power of law*. New York: Routledge.

Smith, D. E. 1987. Women's perspective as a radical critique of sociology. In *Feminism and methodology: Social science issues*, edited by S. Harding, 84–96. Bloomington: Indiana University Press.

Solinger, R. 1992. *Wake up, little Susie: Single pregnancy and race before Roe v. Wade*. New York: Routledge.

———. 2001. *Beggars and choosers: How the politics of choice shapes adoption, abortion, and welfare in the United States*. New York: Hill and Wang.

Stacey, J., and B. Thorne. 1985. The missing feminist revolution in sociology. *Social Problems* 32: 301–316.

Stanton, E. C. 1848. Address delivered at Seneca Falls. In *Elizabeth Cady Stanton/ Susan B. Anthony: Correspondence, writings, speeches*, edited by E. C. DuBois, 27–35. New York: Schocken Books.

Stetson, D. M., ed. 2001. *Abortion politics, women's movements, and the democratic state: A comparative study of state feminism*. Oxford, U.K.: Oxford University Press.

Stevens, J. 1999. *Reproducing the state*. Princeton, N.J.: Princeton University Press.

Stivers, C. 2000. *Bureau men, settlement women: Constructing public administration in the Progressive Era*. Lawrence: University of Kansas Press.

Therborn, G. 1978. *What does the ruling class do when it rules?* London: Verso.

Thorne, B. 1993. *Gender play: Girls and boys in school*. New Brunswick, N.J.: Rutgers University Press.

Tice, K. W. 1998. *Tales of wayward girls and immoral women: Case records and the professionalization of social work*. Urbana: University of Illinois Press.

Uggen, C., and J. Manza. 2002. Democratic contraction? Political consequences of felon disenfranchisement in the United States. *American Sociological Review* 67: 777–803.

Van Ausdale, D., and J. Feagin. 2001. *The first R: How children learn race and racism*. Lanham, Md.: Rowman & Littlefield.

Walkowitz, D. J. 1999. *Working with class: Social workers and the politics of middle-class identity*. Chapel Hill: University of North Carolina Press.

Wallerstein, I. 1974. *The modern world-system: Capitalist agriculture and the origins of the European world-economy in the sixteenth century*. New York: Academic Press.

Weber, M. 1978. *Economy and society*. Berkeley: University of California Press.

———. 1998. *The Protestant ethic and the spirit of capitalism*. Second Roxbury Edition, translated by T. Parsons and introduced by R. Collins. Los Angeles: Roxbury Publishing Co.

Weiss, E. 2000. *Surviving domestic violence: Voices of women who broke free*. Salt Lake City, Utah: Agreka Books.

Weldon, S. L. 2002. *Protest, policy and the problem of violence against women: A cross national comparison*. Pittsburgh, Pa.: University of Pittsburgh Press.

West, C., and S. Fenstermaker. 1995. Doing difference. *Gender and Society* 9: 8–37.

West, C., and D. H. Zimmerman. 1987. Doing gender. *Gender and Society* 1: 125–151.

Williams, C. L., ed. 1993. *Doing "women's work": Men in nontraditional occupations*. Newbury Park, Calif.: Sage Publications.

Wolchik, S. 1989. Women and the state in Eastern Europe and the Soviet Union. In *Women, the state, and development*, edited by S. E. M. Charlton, J. Everett, and K. Staudt, 44–65. Albany: State University of New York Press.

Woolf, V. 1938. *Three guineas*. First American edition. New York: Harcourt, Brace and Co.

Wright, E. O. 1978. *Class, crisis, and the state*. London: Verso.

———. 2002. The shadow of exploitation in Weber's class analysis. *American Sociological Review* 67: 832–853.

Yuval-Davis, N. 1987. Front and rear: The sexual division of labour in the Israeli army. In *Women, state, and ideology: Studies from Africa and Asia*, edited by H. Afshar, 186–204. Albany: State University of New York Press.

Lisa D. Brush teaches sociology and women's studies at the University of Pittsburgh.